serves
one

super meals for solo cooks

serves
one

toni lydecker

LAKE ISLE PRESS NEW YORK

All inquiries should be addressed to:
Lake Isle Press, Inc., 2095 Broadway, Suite 404,
New York, NY 10023

Distributed to the trade by:
National Book Network, Inc., 4720 Boston Way,
Lanham, MD 20706. Phone: 1 800 462 6420

Library of Congress Catalogue
Card Number: 98-65710
ISBN: 1-891105-01-9

Book design by Ellen Swandiak
Illustrations by Piyawat Pattanapuckdee

April 1998
October 1999
10 9 8 7 6 5 4 3 2

First Edition

to Kent, Kate, and Mary

acknowledgments

I wish to thank Hiroko Kiiffner of Lake Isle Press for the intelligence, expertise, and good humor she brought to our collaboration on this cookbook.

I am grateful to Ellen Swandiak for her imaginative design and to Piyawat Pattanapuckdee for his charming illustrations. Thanks to Victoria Mathews for careful and thoughtful editing, and to Sydney W. Cohen for a well-done index.

Special thanks to the many good cooks who shared recipes, practical hints, and stories about solo cooking. They are credited on the pages in which their contributions appear. I am equally indebted to members of my cooking-for-one class, who cheerfully cooked on command and let me know which recipes were keepers.

More thanks to Helen Lydecker, my mother-in-law, for her encouragement and recipe testing, and to Joyce and Carroll Hudson, my parents, for their love and unfailing interest in my work. Pattie Davis, my aunt, not only urged me on but tested several single-serving recipes in her toaster oven. Thanks also to Kate and Mary Lydecker, my daughters, whose pleasure in solo dining was a daily inspiration.

Finally, I want to thank my husband, Kent Lydecker, for support in every sense of the word.

contents

Introduction

Serves One is a cookbook for anyone who eats alone at least some of the time. That includes just about all of us, I suspect.

When I tell others about the book, the response is, quite often, to mention its suitability for people who live alone. I do hope that *Serves One* will be well-thumbed by college graduates moving into their first apartments, newly divorced and widowed people learning to cook or to downsize, retirees with more time to experiment in the kitchen, and seasoned cooks looking for new single-serving ideas.

But solo cooking skills are useful, as well, for those who live in a larger household. Though there are four in my own family, conflicting schedules often prevent us from eating together. Weekday lunches and snacks are almost invariably solo events. As for dinner, if one teenaged daughter is playing basketball, the other heads out for a baby-sitting job, and my husband has a dinner meeting, I am on my own for that meal, as well.

A depressing prospect? In general, no. It's a chance to indulge myself, curling up with a book, a glass of wine, and my favorite salad (Cobb), sandwich (fried egg), or quick soup (garlic). In talking to others, I have found that everyone has their little solo rituals, which might involve whipping up some scrambled eggs late at night or heading for the bathtub with a dinner tray. We hear a lot about eating as a communal experience, but the pleasures of solitary dining are not to be overlooked.

Of course, you have to make something good, and that can be frustrating. "Family-size" food packaging and recipes that produce too much food can be daunting. That's where *Serves One* can help. Most recipes make just one serving and, in deference to the fact that the solo cook is also the cleanup crew, most are quick and simple.

Originally, I thought this would be a strictly single-portion cookbook. But there are undeniable advantages to making some foods, such as a batch of soup, in larger quantities. When that is true, the recipes explain how to divide and package the extra servings for other meals.

Recipes are grouped informally, reflecting the way people like to eat when they are on their own. There are many all-in-one meals, ranging from main-course salads to simple stir-fries to bean-and-rice combos. Other chapters tell how to make easy and appealing pizzas, quick homemade soups, dinner sandwiches, and a few irresistible treats.

Some recipes from other solo cooks are straightforward while others are delightfully idiosyncratic, but all fit into busy lives. One cook likes to start dinner and let it cook while she showers. Another makes and eats dinner while he watches a news show. A third throws together a late, light meal after her daily workout.

Profiles and anecdotes give glimpses of these cooks' interests and personalities, as expressed in the food they make just for themselves. Their styles of cooking, from precise to improvisational, and their tastes for foods as diverse as ratatouille, chili, and Chinese stir-fry, show the rich possibilities open to all of us.

Buying and Storing Ingredients

If you enjoy cooking and eating more than shopping, take time to figure out a game plan for buying ingredients and stocking the kitchen with meal-ready staples.

You'll avoid a lot of aggravation if you find food vendors who will let you order exactly what you need: a butcher who will sell one lamb chop, a deli worker willing to slice three pieces of Swiss, a fishmonger who cheerfully wraps up six scallops. Even in supermarkets that prepackage such products, you can usually get the right quantity just by asking. Individually Quick Frozen (IQF) products such as fish fillets also work well for the single-portion cook.

When a "family size" package of chicken breasts is priced lower, go ahead and buy it. At home, divide the meat into single portions, reserve one to cook, and slip the others into recloseable plastic bags for freezing.

Stock your kitchen with preserved foods such as dried mushrooms, Dijon mustard, capers, and chile oil. Don't worry about using these convenient flavor boosters right away— they have a long shelf life.

You can have a varied assortment of ingredients such as grains and spices if you buy them in small quantities and give some thought to storage. Keep them tightly sealed in the pantry, or freeze them, to avoid worries about deterioration, loss of flavor, or insect invasions.

Because it is shelf stable, dry white vermouth is nice to have on hand when you need a splash of wine in a stew or sauce; its gentle hints of herbs and spices are a bonus. A shallot is often just the right size for a single-serving recipe, allowing you to avoid using only part of an onion; with their distinctive flavor, shallots sometimes can stand in for garlic as well as onion.

The following staples are good to have on hand for your own creations, as well as for the recipes in *Serves One*.

Pantry
- Beans and legumes, dried or canned: chickpeas, black beans, cannellini or other white beans, red or brown lentils

- Eggs: large, in a 6- or 8-egg carton

- Fruit, dried: cranberries or cherries, raisins or currants

- Grains: long-grain white rice (regular American or basmati), short-grain rice such as Italian Arborio, brown rice, bulgur, couscous, stone-ground cornmeal, popcorn

- Mushrooms, dried: porcini, shiitakes, morels, or cloud ears

- Pasta and noodles, dried: long (spaghetti, egg noodles, soba) and short (penne, farfalle)

- Oils: extra-virgin olive oil, unsalted butter, vegetable oil (preferably canola), sesame oil

- Seasonings: table salt for baking and kosher salt for everything else, black peppercorns, white peppercorns, bay leaves, ground red pepper, basil, red pepper flakes, oregano, rosemary, sesame seeds, reduced-sodium soy sauce, vanilla

- Seafood, canned: tuna, salmon, clams, sardines

- Onion family: onions, shallots, garlic

- Tomato-based pasta sauce: ready-made

- Vinegars: white wine, balsamic, rice, malt

- Wines: dry white vermouth, mirin (Japanese sweet rice wine)

Refrigerator
- Bacon or pancetta (unsmoked Italian bacon): by the ounce, from a deli, or buy a larger quantity and freeze some

- Broth concentrate: chicken, beef, vegetable (or, keep canned broth or bouillon cubes in the pantry or homemade broth in the freezer)

- Fruit: lemons and limes, for seasoning; apples, grapes, etc., for snacking

- Hot spice blend: chile oil, curry paste

- Mustard, Dijon: smooth or grainy

- Olives: imported from the Mediterranean, such as Kalamata, Gaeta, niçoise (in a jar, or by the ounce, from a deli)

- Parmesan cheese: preferably Parmigiano-Regglano

- Salad greens

- Scallions

- Tomato paste: in a tube

Freezer
- Breads: whole wheat or white, hard rolls, flour tortillas

- Gingerroot: to be grated as needed

- Nuts: pecans, hazelnuts, almonds, walnuts

Kitchen Tools

An old Chinese saying goes something like this: In times of emergency, one peels potatoes with an ax. The rest of the time, though, it is more efficient and pleasant to have the right tools for cooking small quantities.

Cookware

You'll need a skillet, 8 to 10 inches in diameter, for sautéing and stir frying. You can use what is, strictly speaking, a sauté pan with vertical sides, or it may have sloping sides. Throughout this book, "skillet" is the word used to identify this invaluable piece of cookware.

A ridged "grill" pan of a similar diameter is useful but not essential for cooking a tuna steak or lamb chop. A 6- or 7-inch skillet, just large enough to toast a few nuts or fry an egg, also falls in the nice-but-optional category. If you own more than one skillet, one could be made of cast iron, or have a nonstick cooking surface.

A small saucepan, roughly twice as wide as it is deep, is very handy for cooking or reheating single servings: 1 1/2 quarts is a good size, and it should have a cover. A large saucepan holding 5 or 6 quarts is ideal for cooking pasta and making soups.

A medium-size saucepan (about 3 quarts) is useful but not essential. Some solo cooks like to use a flat-bottomed wok as a dual-purpose substitute for a medium-size skillet and saucepan.

Your cookware should be made of heavy-duty nonreactive metal, such as anodized aluminum or stainless steel with a layer of heat-conducting aluminum in the base (an exception to this rule would be a cast iron skillet, which is indestructible and wonderful for cooking, but may react with acidic foods). Buy the best quality you can and the cookware will last a lifetime, or close to it.

Knives

The three knives I use all the time are a paring knife, a 10-inch cook's knife for chopping and slicing, and a serrated knife for cutting breads and tomatoes.

Appliances

A blender is helpful in making pureed soups and smoothies. A food processor is recommended for a few recipes, but it is not an essential piece of equipment. For soups and most other items, you could just as well use an old-fashioned food mill, which purees and strains in one motion.

You can trust a microwave to thaw and reheat foods efficiently, and to perform small chores such as melting butter. It also does a good job of cooking some vegetables, "poaching" a fish or chicken fillet, and cooking rice. When the microwave produces food of quality equal to that produced on top of the stove, I offer directions. If you are buying a microwave, you might consider a model that doubles as a convection oven.

A toaster oven is quite useful for single-portion cooking. You can use it to toast a sandwich or make a solo pizza, among other things. For items that are larger or denser—the Mini Meat Loaf, say—you are better off using a conventional oven.

Other Handy Items

Small ceramic gratin dishes, holding 1 to 2 cups, are great for making oven-baked casseroles.

A digital scale is an aid not only in weighing ingredients, but in tracking the portion sizes you are eating. For use in freezing single servings, lay in a supply of plastic microwaveable containers in 1- and 2-cup sizes and some self-stick labels.

Also useful for solo cooking are: a colander, a strainer, a couple of wooden spoons, a pair of pincer-type tongs, an instant-read thermometer to check food temperatures, 1-quart recloseable plastic bags for marinating a tuna steak or chicken breast, and a small cheese grater to hold over a pasta or soup bowl.

7

SALADS

Whether I am making a meal-size extravaganza with all my favorite ingredients, or just a little salad to go with something else, I try to start with nice greens. If Boston lettuce looks fresh and unblemished, that's what I buy, even if my list calls for romaine. Keeping two complementary kinds of greens on hand works even better—there is no easier way to make a salad look and taste more interesting.

On that leafy foundation, I can build almost anything. There are some combinations, such as the spinach Cobb and Greek salad recipes in this chapter, that I go back to over and over. Other salads are inspired by whatever turns up in the pantry and refrigerator. Raw vegetables, fresh or dried fruit, and nuts or seeds are some obvious candidates. If I run across something more substantial—a few spears of lightly cooked asparagus, the remains of last night's salmon fillet or wild rice pilaf, a sautéed chicken breast—I know that my meal preparations are almost complete.

Greens Glossary

name	flavor	lasts	pair with
arugula	dark green; tender; bitter	three days or less	Bibb, Boston, or other tender lettuces
Belgian endive	long, smooth, pale green leaves; bitter	one week or longer	any mild, darker green
Boston or bibb	light green; tender texture; delicate flavor	1 week or less	mesclun, baby spinach, arugula
escarole	medium green; crunchy; slightly bitter	1 to 2 weeks	red-tipped or green leaf lettuce, iceberg
iceberg	light green; very crunchy; mild flavor	1 to 2 weeks	leaf lettuce, spinach, radicchio
leaf lettuce	medium green or red-tipped; tender; delicate flavor	1 week or less	watercress or another piquant green
mesclun	Mixed baby and specialty greens, sold by the ounce or packaged; varied flavors and textures	3 days or less	Boston lettuce or other tender greens
radicchio	Purplish-red; crisp; bitter	1 to 2 weeks	romaine, iceberg, any leaf lettuce
sprouts (radish, alfalfa, Mung, etc.)	white to dark green; slightly crunchy; piquant	3 days or less	spinach or any leaf lettuce
watercress	Dark green, circular leaves; piquant, peppery taste	1 week or less	leaf lettuce, Boston or Bibb

Salad Strategies

Choosing Greens

• Pair a mild-tasting green with a more strongly flavored one, in a two-to-one ratio. Or, combine pale greens with vitamin-rich dark greens.

• Buy greens in small quantities for quick use. Baby escarole, mixed spring greens (mesclun) sold by the ounce, and Boston lettuce are well-sized for the single-portion cook. With the produce manager's permission, break off part of a too-large clump of chicory or escarole (make sure it is sold by the pound, not the head).

• Prewashed spinach may be worth buying because it is such a pain to clean. This is also a good way to buy a small quantity of mixed greens.

Cleaning Greens

• At home, transfer unwashed greens to a perforated plastic "vegetable bag" or wrap in paper towels before refrigerating.

• To clean, immerse greens in water; lift, and drain in a colander or salad spinner. Change the water and repeat until no soil is left behind. Drain thoroughly and wrap the greens in paper towels or a clean kitchen towel. Cleaned and dried in this way, romaine and other sturdy greens keep several days. If greens are more delicate, clean only the amount you plan to use that day.

• Leave prewashed greens in their package until needed. Once the package is opened, use the greens within a day or two.

From the Salad Bar

• Freshly made, mixed greens may be a good deal. Or, take home a little red cabbage or spinach to combine with the romaine in your refrigerator.

• Tired of finding a limp head of celery or moldy cucumber at the bottom of your vegetable crisper? Try buying problem ingredients by the ounce—chopped, sliced, or shredded.

• If you want just a few artichoke hearts, chickpeas, or olives, buy them by the ounce at a salad bar or deli counter.

• If the salad bar offers a housemade dressing that you love, fill a small container to use for several days.

Crisp Toppings and More

Bacon Bits

Fry 1 bacon strip in a small skillet until crisp; drain off the fat and crumble the bacon.

Croutons

Cut any hearty, European-style bread (preferably stale) into cubes, leaving the crusts on. If the bread cubes feel soft or moist, heat them in a small skillet, over the lowest setting, until they feel dry.

If the bread has a lot of personality or contains oil, the croutons may taste fine as they are. Otherwise, flavor them as follows:

● Remove the bread cubes from the pan. Add a little extra-virgin olive oil and a clove or two of crushed garlic to the pan, raise the heat, and cook until the garlic turns golden.

● Remove the garlic and return the croutons to the pan. Sprinkle with dried thyme, oregano, rosemary, or a seasoning blend.

● Cook the cubes, turning them occasionally and checking often to prevent burning. Remove from the heat when they are crisp and have turned golden.

Toasted Nuts and Seeds

Toast pecans, walnuts, or almonds over medium-low heat in a small skillet or in a 300-degree oven for 10 to 15 minutes, until lightly browned and crisp. Sesame seeds or sunflower seeds take less time, about 5 minutes. To deepen the flavor of nuts and seeds, coat them in a little vegetable oil before toasting.

Salad Dressing

By making your own dressing, one portion at a time, you can control the quality and proportions of ingredients, matching them to your salad du jour. If you use a prepared dressing, instead, choose an all-natural product made with olive oil or a polyunsaturated oil such as canola, safflower or soybean.

Flavor Boosters

Other easy ways to make a single-portion salad taste special:

● Rub crushed garlic over the salad plate, or add it to a premixed dressing.

● Sprinkle on parsley leaves or other fresh herbs.

● Add bits of a strongly flavored cheese such as Gorgonzola, feta, or Roquefort.

One salad may need a little more dressing or a little less than another, and personal tastes can vary. Find a formula that suits you, using this recipe to get started.

Basic Vinaigrette

A large pinch of kosher salt
Dash of freshly ground black pepper
1 tablespoon extra-virgin olive oil
**1 teaspoon vinegar (balsamic, red wine, sherry, cider, herb-
flavored, etc.)**

1 Ad hoc method: Place the greens in a large bowl, sprinkle with the oil, and toss the salad. Sprinkle with the vinegar, and toss again. Add the salt and pepper, and give the salad a final toss.

2 Premixed method: Measure the oil, vinegar, salt, and pepper into a small jar with a lid or a squeeze bottle. Cover and shake vigorously. Drizzle over the salad and toss.

Cook's Note

Using a bowl about twice the size of the ingredients makes it easier to toss the salad.

variations

Mustard: 1 tablespoon extra-virgin olive or canola oil, 1 teaspoon balsamic vinegar, a dab of coarse or smooth Dijon mustard

Berry: 1 tablespoon extra-virgin olive oil, 1 teaspoon raspberry vinegar, salt, freshly ground black pepper

Citrus: 1 tablespoon extra-virgin olive oil, 1 to 2 teaspoons lemon, lime or orange juice, salt, freshly ground black pepper

When I'm by myself and feeling lazy, I use a Pyrex pie plate both for mixing and eating this salad.

Spinach Cobb Salad

Makes 1 serving Prep: 15 minutes

2 cups spinach and sprouts, or other mixed greens

1/2 cup cooked, cubed chicken (see Note)

1/4 avocado, cubed

3 white button mushrooms, sliced

4 cherry tomatoes, cut in half, or 1 small tomato, cut into bite-
size pieces

2 tablespoons Basic Vinaigrette (page 14), or mustard variation
(page 14)

1 strip crisply cooked bacon, crumbled

1 Combine the spinach and sprouts, chicken, avocado, mushrooms and tomatoes.

2 Add the vinaigrette and toss the salad. Top with the bacon.

Cook's Notes

● Cut out only the avocado section you need, leaving the skin on the rest; rub the cut surface with lemon juice, cover tightly with plastic wrap and refrigerate up to 2 days. Use the remainder in salads or make a quick guacamole by mashing the avocado with a little salsa, salt, and lime juice.

● Use leftover chicken. Or, moisten a skinless, boneless chicken breast half with 2 tablespoons broth or water, cover, and microwave at full power until cooked through, about 3 minutes.

Asian-Style Chicken Salad

Makes 1 serving   Prep: 10 minutes, plus marinating time
Cook: 10 minutes

2 teaspoons grated gingerroot

2 teaspoons finely chopped garlic

1 tablespoon mirin (Japanese sweet rice wine), or sweet sherry

1 tablespoon reduced-sodium soy sauce

1 tablespoon toasted sesame oil

1 skinless, boneless chicken breast half

1/2 red or yellow bell pepper, cut into thin strips

1 1/2 to 2 cups Boston lettuce and watercress, or other mixed
    greens, torn into bite-sized pieces

1 teaspoon vegetable oil

1 Put the gingerroot and garlic in a 1-quart recloseable plastic bag. Measure the mirin, soy sauce, and sesame oil into the bag. Massage the bag lightly to mix the ingredients.

2 Using a meat pounder or a small, heavy saucepan, flatten the chicken fillet to an even thickness. Put the fillet inside the bag and seal it, forcing out air. Turn the bag several times to coat the fillet. Marinate at least half an hour or, in the refrigerator, as long as 8 hours.

3 Ten minutes before eating, scatter the salad greens on a dinner plate. Heat the vegetable oil over medium-high heat in a small skillet or ridged grill pan (preferably nonstick). Cook the pepper strips, turning occasionally, until softened and slightly charred; set aside.

4 Brown the chicken fillet on both sides, reduce heat to medium, and cook until the center is no longer pink, about 5 minutes. Transfer the fillet to a clean cutting board and let it rest several minutes. Add 1/2 cup water to the pan and cook a minute or two longer, stirring.

5 Slice the chicken on an angle into strips and place in the center of the greens. Drizzle the pan juices over the meat and scatter the pepper strips on top.

Undressed greens taste refreshingly cool and crisp against the vibrant ginger-garlic flavoring of the chicken.

This nourishing and robust salad makes a good hot-weather meal because you don't need to turn on the stove. Eat it with pita triangles or sourdough bread.

Chickpea and Tuna Salad

Makes 1 generous serving   Prep: 10 minutes

One 3-ounce can tuna, drained

1 cup chickpeas (half one 19-ounce can), drained and rinsed

1 scallion, including most of the green part, chopped

2 tablespoons chopped red bell pepper (raw or roasted)

2 to 4 imported black olives, such as Kalamata or niçoise, pitted and sliced

1 1/2 tablespoons extra-virgin olive oil

1 tablespoon lemon juice

Salt to taste

Red pepper flakes or freshly ground black pepper

Torn romaine and radicchio leaves, or other mixed salad greens

1 Combine the tuna, chickpeas, scallion, bell pepper, olives, olive oil, and lemon juice in a bowl. Taste, and add salt if needed (remember that the tuna and olives contain sodium). Add red pepper flakes to taste.

2 Line a dinner plate with greens, and spoon the chickpea-tuna mixture on top.

Cook's Note

Refrigerated, without the salad greens, this salad will keep a couple of days.

Leftovers make a good brown-bag lunch, packed in a plastic container or spooned into pita pockets.

Tabbouli

Makes 1 large serving   Prep: 15 minutes, plus soaking time

1/2 cup bulgur
1/2 cup chopped fresh parsley
2 tablespoons chopped fresh mint (optional)
1 scallion, with most of the green part, chopped
1 small tomato, peeled and chopped
2 tablespoons extra-virgin olive oil
2 tablespoons lemon juice
1/4 teaspoon salt
Mixed, torn greens

1 Put the bulgur in a small bowl and pour 1/2 cup of boiling water over it. Cover and set aside for 15 to 20 minutes. Drain thoroughly in a strainer and fluff gently with a fork.

2 Mix in the parsley, mint, scallion, tomato, olive oil, lemon juice, and salt. Let stand at least 1 hour for flavors to blend. Serve on a bed of mixed greens.

Goat cheese, pecans, and dried cranberries are an irresistible triad, as this salad demonstrates.

Goat Cheese on Greens

Makes 1 serving   Prep: 15 minutes

1 large slice goat cheese (about 1 1/2 ounces) with chives or mixed herbs

2 tablespoons Basic Vinaigrette (page 14), made with white wine vinegar

2 cups mesclun, or other mixed greens

6 toasted pecans or walnuts (page 13)

1 tablespoon dried cranberries

1 Shape the goat cheese into a disk about 1 inch thick and place in a small, ovenproof dish. Drizzle 1 tablespoon of vinaigrette over the cheese.

2 In an oven set on warm, heat the cheese until it softens a little but does not lose its shape, about 10 minutes.

3 Toss the mesclun with the remaining tablespoon of dressing, and transfer to a dinner plate. Place the goat cheese in the center, and scatter the pecans and cranberries on top.

Greek Salad

Makes 1 serving   Prep: 15 minutes

1 medium tomato or 6 cherry tomatoes

1/2 medium cucumber, peeled

2 to 4 imported black olives, such as Kalamata or niçoise,
  pitted and slivered

2 tablespoons crumbled feta cheese

2 or 3 torn romaine leaves

2 teaspoons extra-virgin olive oil

2 teaspoons lemon juice

1/4 teaspoon dried oregano

Salt and freshly ground black pepper to taste

1 Cut the tomato into bite-size pieces, or halve the cherry tomatoes. Halve the cucumber vertically and, if you like, scrape out the seeds with a spoon; cut into bite-size pieces.

2 Combine the olives with the tomato, cucumber, feta cheese, and romaine on a salad plate or in a bowl. Sprinkle the olive oil, lemon juice, oregano, and salt and pepper over the salad and mix gently.

The popularity of the Caesar may come and go, but my teenaged daughter's loyalty never wavers. Kate will assemble one for a solo lunch, mid-afternoon snack, or dinner as long as the romaine supply holds out.

A homemade Caesar dressing calls for half a dozen ingredients—and then there's the dilemma of raw egg, cooked egg or no egg. The easy way out is to use a good, all-natural bottled dressing. Kate is partial to Paul Newman's Caesar Dressing, a vinaigrette.

You can use ready-made croutons—in fact, I've seen "Caesar salad kits" in the supermarket—but, if you have some good bread on hand, you can make your own in minutes (page 13).

Easy Caesar

Makes 1 serving Prep: 10 minutes

1 1/2 to 2 cups chopped romaine, including some tender inner leaves
2 tablespoons bottled Caesar salad dressing
1/2 to 1 cup croutons
4 Parmesan shavings, made with a vegetable peeler
1 or 2 sweet onion slices (optional)

1 Toss the romaine with the Caesar dressing.

2 Top the salad with the croutons, Parmesan shavings, and optional onion slices.

variation

Chicken Caesar Salad: For a meal-size salad, lightly pound a skinless, boneless chicken breast half to a uniform thickness and marinate in 1 tablespoon of Caesar salad dressing. Sauté in a small, heavy skillet. Transfer the cooked fillet to the center of the dressed greens and surround with the remaining ingredients.

This refreshing and virtually fat-free salad belongs to the Japanese category of dishes known as *sunomono* ("vinegared things"). The dressing can also be mixed with tomato, cucumber, and sweet onion slices—not a traditional Japanese combination, but delicious nonetheless.

Marinated Cucumbers and Radishes

Makes 1 serving Prep: 10 minutes, plus marinating time

1/2 medium cucumber, peeled and seeded
5 medium radishes, trimmed
2 tablespoons natural rice vinegar
1/2 teaspoon sugar
1/2 teaspoon salt

1 Using a sharp knife, cut the cucumber and radishes into very thin slices. Place in 2 small bowls, or well-separated in a single bowl (to prevent the vinegar-dressed radishes from "bleeding" onto the cucumber).

2 Mix together the rice vinegar, sugar, and salt. Gently mix the dressing with the cucumber and radish slices. Marinate 1 to 12 hours; combine the vegetables just before eating.

Cook's Note

Speed tip: For the dressing, substitute 2 tablespoons of seasoned rice vinegar, which already contains sugar and salt.

Roasting brings out the sweet, earthy flavor of beets. You won't want to crank up the oven for two beets, but why not pop them in with a Mini Meat Loaf (page 84) or roast Rock Cornish Hen (page 83)? The sharp taste of bitter greens is nice with beets, but if you prefer milder greens, so be it.

Roasted Beets with Bitter Greens

Makes 1 serving   Prep: 10 minutes Cook: 40 minutes

2 small beets, or 1 large beet

2 tablespoons Mustard Vinaigrette, made with orange juice (page 14)

1 1/2 cups bitter greens, such as watercress or curly chicory

1 Cut the beets in half and place the cut sides down in a shallow baking dish. Roast in an oven set at 350-400 degrees until the beets are tender when pierced with a knife (about 40 minutes). Remove from the oven and, while the beets are still warm, strip off the skins. Cut the beets into cubes, and mix with 1 tablespoon of the dressing.

2 Toss the greens with the remaining tablespoon of dressing and transfer to a salad plate. Heap the beet cubes on top.

Cook's Note

As an alternative to roasting, steam the beets on top of the stove until tender.

Lazy Picnic Ways

the French root of the word *picnique* means "to pick a trifle." But that hardly does justice to the Gallic genius for open-air dining.

It is easy to picnic as the French do, insists Josyane Colwell, who grew up in Provence but now is chef/owner of Le Moulin, a gourmet take-out and catering business in the Hudson River Valley. Just start with the basics. "You'd never catch a French person without a baguette, cheese and wine," says Josy.

The French have the good sense to relax while picnicking. Instead of grilling, they pack wonderful cold delicacies. You might take a slice of thick, baked ham, roast veal or pâté from a good deli, well-chilled melon slices or pears, and perhaps a little Brie or Roquefort for dessert.

Add a homemade salad, such as Josy's green bean salad, and you have the makings of a fresh-air feast—even if it takes place on your own terrace or by an open window.

Josy's Green Bean Salad

Makes 1 serving   Prep: 15 minutes Cook: 5 minutes

1/3 pound haricots verts (or any small, tender green beans), trimmed

3 medium white mushrooms, sliced

1 ounce semi-soft pecorino or Gruyère cheese, cut into matchsticks

1 teaspoon chopped red onion (optional)

1 1/2 tablespoons extra-virgin olive oil

1 tablespoon cider or white wine vinegar

1/8 teaspoon grainy Dijon mustard

Salt and freshly ground pepper to taste

1 Boil the green beans in abundant salted water until tender but still crisp, about 2 minutes; drain and cool under running water.

2 Combine the beans with the mushrooms and cheese in a plastic container (for picnicking) or on a salad plate. Top with chopped red onion, if you like.

3 Combine the oil, vinegar, mustard, and salt and pepper in a small jar or squeeze bottle, and shake. Shortly before eating, drizzle the dressing over the salad and mix gently.

SOUPS

A cache of homemade soup tucked away in the refrigerator or freezer gives me the same smug feeling as money in the bank. Maybe it's even better—after all, I can't heat up cold cash for dinner.

Making a batch of soup almost always pays off. When you come home tired, it's nice to dip out a bowlful or thaw a single serving. These recipes make a fairly small quantity—two or three quarts—so you won't tire of the soup before it's gone. Other soups can be assembled and cooked so quickly that making just one or two servings isn't a big deal.

In all recipes, whether for a small quantity or a larger batch, a meal-size single serving consists of two cups of soup.

Your meal in a bowl can be made entirely from fresh ingredients and your own homemade broth. Or, you can get good results by combining fresh ingredients with frozen, dried, or canned ingredients. Cooks short on time should turn to the "Almost-Instant Soups" at the end of the chapter.

You can use any small or medium-size saucepan to make the single-portion soups. To make soup by the batch, you will need a larger saucepan or stockpot— possibly the same one you use to cook pasta. Ideally, the bottom of your soup pot should be heavy, to prevent burning, and fairly broad, for recipes that begin with sautéing some ingredients.

This light and delicious soup is a bright green, not the familiar khaki green of split-pea soup. Barbara Carmenini, a caterer in Irvington, New York, gave me the recipe.

Green Pea Soup

Makes 1 serving Prep: 15 minutes Cook: 20 minutes

1 tablespoon vegetable oil

1 small leek, cleaned (see Note) and sliced

1 to 1 1/2 cups chicken broth

1 cup frozen green peas

1 large, fresh mint leaf, torn or cut in ribbons (optional)

1 Heat the oil over medium-high heat in a small, heavy saucepan and cook the leek until tender. Add 1 cup of the chicken broth and the peas. When the mixture begins to boil, reduce the heat to medium and simmer about 10 minutes.

2 Puree the mixture in a blender (see Notes) or food processor until fairly smooth; if it seems too thick, add the remaining half cup of broth. Add the mint if using, just before you eat.

Cook's Notes

• To clean the leek, cut off the root end and the tough green leaves, leaving behind the white bulb and tender, pale green leaves. Cut the leek in half, lengthwise, and immerse in water, swishing back and forth to loosen dirt. Replace the water and repeat until no grit remains behind.

• Blenders do a great job of pureeing soup, but if the soup is too hot, there is a small but real chance that the pressure of the steam will blow off the container top. As precautions, allow the soup to cool at least 10 minutes, and fill the container no more than half full.

Garlic Queen and Soup Lover

t he first time Pat Reppert staged a garlic festival, in New York's Catskills Mountains, about a hundred people showed up to admire the herbs in her greenhouse and to taste her good and garlicky home cooking. At last count, attendance for the annual event was up to 45,000. Pat long ago turned the festival over to the local Kiwanis Club, but she remains chief organizer and, with her garlic clove earrings and hats, the undisputed queen of garlic.

A woman with more than one mission, Pat also hosts a five-minute cooking program for a nearby radio station. "I want people to realize that cooking is a creative activity," she says. To that end, she supplies easy recipes and practical tips aimed at luring them into the kitchen.

Many of Pat's recipes call for garlic or fresh herbs, if not both. She recommends making a batch of garlic broth and freezing some in individual portions, to use in making all kinds of soups. If you think you're catching a cold, she swears you can kick it by sipping hot garlic broth with lots of fresh ginger grated into it. Frozen herb cubes and butter are two other examples of what Pat calls "aromatherapy in the kitchen."

Herb Cubes: Combine 2 cups of basil, parsley, or another favorite herb with 2 cloves of finely chopped garlic, up to 1/2 cup water, and 3 tablespoons extra-virgin olive oil. Puree the mixture, and spoon into mini ice cube trays. Use a cube to season a portion of soup, spaghetti, or steamed vegetables.

Herb Butter: Soften a stick of butter at room temperature, and, using a fork, blend in 1 to 2 tablespoons of finely chopped herbs and garlic. Form into a log, wrap in several layers of plastic wrap, and freeze. To use the butter, slice off the amount you need (as little as half a teaspoon will do the trick) and return the rest to the freezer. Set the flavored butter pat on a fish fillet before broiling, slip it into microwaved peas just before they're done, or use it to "help out" a canned soup.

Garlic and Ginger Soup

Makes 1 serving   Prep: 10 minutes Cook: 30 minutes

variations

Tortilla Soup: Omit the gingerroot, vinegar, and soy sauce; add 1 fresh or canned tomato to the other ingredients. After straining the broth, add 1/2 cup chicken cubes and simmer until done.

After spooning the soup into your bowl, add 2 tablespoons crumbled farmer's cheese or goat's cheese, a taco shell broken into bits (or a handful of crushed corn tortilla chips), and a squeeze of fresh lime.

Tortellini-Spinach Soup: Omit the vinegar, soy sauce and Tabasco. After straining the broth, return it to the saucepan.

Add 1/2 cup dried, fresh, or frozen tortellini and 1 cup shredded spinach leaves; simmer until the tortellini are cooked.

3 1/2 cups chicken broth or All-Purpose Meat Broth (page 41)

1 tablespoon coarsely grated gingerroot

4 peeled garlic cloves

1 celery stalk, trimmed and cut into chunks

1 carrot, trimmed and cut into chunks

1/2 teaspoon balsamic or cider vinegar

1 teaspoon reduced-sodium soy sauce

Dash of Tabasco sauce

Finely chopped fresh parsley or cilantro (optional)

1 Combine the chicken broth, gingerroot, garlic, celery, and carrot in a medium-size saucepan. Bring the mixture to a boil, reduce the heat to low, and simmer 30 minutes. Pour through a fine-meshed strainer into a bowl.

2 Stir in the vinegar, soy sauce, and Tabasco. Sprinkle with the parsley or cilantro (if using).

31

This easy-sipping soup is for days when it is too hot to cook.

Cucumber-Yogurt Soup

Makes 1 serving   **Prep: 10 minutes, plus chilling time**

1 small cucumber (peel only if the skin is waxed), sliced
1/2 small onion, sliced
1 cup chicken broth
1/2 cup yogurt
1 dill sprig (optional)
Salt to taste

1 Combine the cucumber, onion, chicken broth, yogurt, and dill (if using) in a blender container. Blend at high speed until all ingredients are liquified.

2 Taste and add salt (blending briefly) if needed. Pour the soup into a large mug and chill at least 2 hours.

Kale and Kielbasa Soup

Makes 2 servings   **Prep: 15 minutes**   **Cook: 30 minutes**

4 1/2 cups chicken broth or All-Purpose Meat Broth (page 41)
1 finely chopped garlic clove
1/2 cup chopped onion
1/2 cup diced carrot
1/2 cup sliced celery
2 or 3 pieces kale, shredded
1/2 cup kielbasa (Polish sausage) cubes
Salt and freshly ground pepper to taste

1 Combine the chicken broth, garlic, onion, carrot, celery, kale, and kielbasa in a medium-size saucepan, and bring to a boil. Reduce the heat to medium-low, and cover.

2 Simmer 30 minutes, until all ingredients are tender. Taste and season with salt and pepper.

Japanese buckwheat noodles, heated in a fragrant broth, make a nourishing soup.

Soba Noodles in Broth

Makes 1 serving Prep: 10 minutes Cook: 10 minutes

2 tablespoons reduced-sodium soy sauce

2 tablespoons mirin (Japanese sweet rice wine)

2 teaspoons sugar

1/4 teaspoon instant dashi granules (see Note)

3 ounces dried soba noodles

1 tablespoon finely chopped scallion, including some of the
   green part

1 In a small saucepan, combine the soy sauce, mirin, and sugar with 1 cup of water, and bring to a boil. Remove from the heat and stir in the dashi granules. Keep the broth warm over a burner set on low.

2 In a medium-size saucepan, bring 1 quart of water to a boil. Stir in the soba noodles and boil until they are cooked but slightly al dente, about 4 minutes. Drain the noodles and transfer them to a soup bowl. Pour the broth over the noodles and sprinkle with the scallion.

Cook's Notes

● Look for soba (buckwheat noodles) and instant dashi granules (dried ground bonito and other seasonings, sold under the name *hon-dashi*) in specialty stores that sell Asian foods; bottled dashi broth can also be used.

● If you cannot find these products, substitute vermicelli for soba and chicken stock for diluted dashi.

variation

Soba Noodles with Shrimp and Snow Peas: Boil 8 snow peas or sugar snap peas in the water (before adding noodles) until tender but still crisp, about 1 minute; lift out with a slotted spoon and set aside.

Simmer 4 to 6 shelled shrimp in the broth until they turn pink, about 30 seconds; remove with the slotted spoon.

Cook the noodles as described in the main recipe. After transferring them to a bowl, arrange the shrimp or chicken and snow peas on top, and pour the broth over them.

This is the soup to eat, hot or cold, when locally grown tomatoes are in season. Its flavor ranges from good to incredibly good, depending on tomato quality.

Fresh Tomato Soup

Makes 1 serving Prep: 10 minutes Cook: 20 minutes

1 teaspoon butter

2 tablespoons finely chopped shallot or onion

2 or 3 ripe, unpeeled tomatoes (1 1/4 pounds), cut into large chunks

1 cup chicken broth or water

Freshly ground white pepper to taste

Salt to taste

2 or 3 fresh basil leaves, torn or cut in ribbons

1 Melt the butter on low heat in a small saucepan. Cook the shallot, covered, until it is translucent. Add the tomatoes, chicken broth, and white pepper; cover and simmer until the tomato pieces are soft.

2 Press the soup through a food mill fitted with a fine sieve, or puree in a blender (see Note) and press through a fine-meshed strainer. Taste and season with salt. Scatter the basil pieces on top.

Cook's Note

If you use a blender, allow the soup to cool at least 10 minutes before pureeing, and fill the container no more than half full.

variations

• When tomatoes are out of season, substitute fresh tomato puree packaged in a shelf-stable aseptic box (Pomì is a good brand) or canned tomatoes imported from Italy. In place of fresh basil, add a sprinkle of dried basil.

• For a richer texture and taste, add 1 or 2 tablespoons of heavy cream.

Caraway seeds and browned onions give this potato soup a hearty flavor that prompts Dina Ebenstein, who gave me the recipe, to call it a "winter soup." Her teenaged grandson has been known to eat it, hot or cold, for every meal until the entire potful is gone.

Hearty Potato Soup

Makes 3 or 4 servings Prep: 20 minutes Cook: 1 hour

3 tablespoons butter

1 large onion, chopped

3 cups peeled and diced potatoes

1 carrot, peeled and grated

1 teaspoon salt

1 tablespoon caraway seeds

2 tablespoons farina (optional) (see Note)

1 cup milk

1/4 cup chopped fresh parsley

1 Melt the butter in a large saucepan (preferably wide-bottomed) over medium heat. Cook the onion until browned (be careful not to burn it). Add the potatoes, carrot, salt, caraway seeds, and enough water to cover the ingredients.

2 Bring the mixture to a boil, reduce the heat, and cook until the potato cubes are tender. Add the farina and cook, stirring often, until the soup thickens. Turn off the heat and stir in the milk and parsley.

Cook's Note

Farina is found in the cereal aisle of your supermarket.

Beef, Barley, and Mushroom Soup

Makes 4 servings   Prep: 20 minutes   Cook: 45 minutes

2 tablespoons vegetable oil

1/2 cup finely chopped onion or shallot

1/2 cup pearled barley

1/8 teaspoon freshly ground black pepper

7 cups All-Purpose Meat Broth (page 41) or beef broth (can be partly water, if the broth is strong)

1/2 pound sirloin tip or another tender beef cut, sliced into strips 1/4 inch thick and 1 inch long

1 cup sliced white button mushrooms

Salt to taste

1 Heat the oil over medium heat in a large, heavy-bottomed saucepan. Cook the onion, barley, and black pepper, stirring often, until the onion is translucent and the barley smells toasty. Add the broth and raise the heat to high.

2 When the broth comes to a boil, add the beef strips and mushrooms, reduce the heat to low, and simmer the soup 30 to 45 minutes. Taste and season with salt.

Mingling several members of the onion family gives this soup a delicate but multidimensional character.

Three-Onion Soup

Makes 3 or 4 servings Prep: 20 minutes Cook: 1 hour

2 tablespoons butter

1 large Spanish onion, sliced (about 4 cups)

2 leeks, cleaned (page 29) and sliced, including some of the
   pale green part (1 1/2 cups)

2 shallots, chopped

2 or 3 garlic cloves, finely chopped

1/4 cup dry white vermouth

4 cups canned beef broth or All-Purpose Meat Broth (page 41),
   plus 2 cups water

1/4 teaspoon dried thyme

1/8 teaspoon freshly ground white pepper

1/2 cup reduced-fat sour cream

Salt to taste

1 Melt the butter in a large saucepan over medium heat. Add the onion, leeks, shallots, and garlic, cover, and cook gently until the onion and garlic are tender but not browned.

2 Raise the heat to medium high, add the vermouth, and cook until it has almost evaporated. Pour in the broth, add the thyme and white pepper, and bring to a boil. Reduce the heat to low and cook, covered, about 1 hour.

3 Blend in the sour cream. Taste and add salt as necessary.

Cook's Note

If you plan to freeze this soup, omit the sour cream. After thawing and heating a single serving, add a tablespoon of sour cream.

Lemony Lentil Soup

Makes 6 servings   Prep: 20 minutes   Cook: 1 to 2 hours

2 medium onions, finely chopped

1 pound dried lentils, rinsed

1 medium carrot, peeled and chopped

1 medium zucchini, peeled and chopped

1/2 cup chopped tomato (fresh or canned)

1 teaspoon ground cumin

1 tablespoon salt

2 tablespoons vegetable oil

1 lemon wedge (per portion)

My mother-in-law, Helen Lydecker, encountered this soup in Egypt and brought back the recipe to make at home in West Texas. Even my husband, formerly a lentil hater, admits that his mom's soup tastes good.

1 Put half of the onions into a large saucepan; set the remainder aside. Add the lentils, carrot, zucchini, tomato, cumin, and salt. Fill with water to a point about two inches above the surface of the lentils. Bring the mixture to a boil, reduce the heat to low, and simmer, partly covered, for an hour or longer, until the lentils and vegetables are tender (check occasionally and add water if necessary). Cool the soup slightly.

2 Puree the soup, in batches, in a food processor or blender (see Note). Return the soup to the pan and keep it warm.

3 Heat the oil in a small skillet, add the remaining onion, and cook until it turns golden brown. Stir the onion into the soup and cook a few minutes longer. Squeeze lemon juice into a soup portion just before eating.

Cook's Notes

● For safety's sake, allow the soup to cool at least 10 minutes before pureeing, and fill the blender container no more than half full.

● For an ultra-velvety texture, strain the soup.

● To freeze single portions, ladle the soup into 2-cup plastic containers, seal tightly, and label.

Time Savers

Almost Instant Soups

When you are rushed, prepared soups come in handy. Luckily, there are more choices—canned, frozen, or dried—than there used to be. I know one busy person who claims to live on Nile dried soups and, after tasting several, I can see why she likes them.

Sometimes just an extra ingredient or two can make a big difference. These single-portion soups take only minutes to make.

Ramen Supreme: Simmer 1 cup frozen stir-fry vegetables in 2 cups chicken or vegetable broth; stir in a package of ramen noodles (discard the flavor packet), and cook 3 minutes longer; sprinkle with soy sauce or stir in a bit of miso.

Lemony Beef Broth: Add a squirt of lemon juice and a dash of Tabasco to 2 cups of hot beef broth; drink the soup from a mug, floating a few oyster crackers on top.

Pasta in Broth: Heat 2 cups chicken or vegetable broth combined with a splash of tomato juice; simmer with a little vermicelli or pastine and 1/2 cup fresh or frozen green beans.

Potluck Gazpacho: Whir last night's Greek or Italian salad in the blender; dilute with tomato juice.

Tomato-Rice Soup: Add a tablespoon of rice or orzo to canned tomato soup, and simmer until tender.

Freezing Single Servings

● Ladle 2 cups cooked soup into separate plastic containers. Seal securely and label with the name of the soup and the date.

● If you are using sturdy, microwaveable containers, such as Rubbermaid or Tupperware, stack them in the freezer. If you are recycling flimsier deli or cottage cheese containers, enclose each one in a recloseable plastic freezer bag for extra protection.

● Thaw soups in the refrigerator or microwave. Or, leave at room temperature just long enough for the soup to loosen from the sides, then slide the contents into a pan for microwaving or heating on a burner.

Broth Basics

The Homemade Kind

Some single-portion cooks make their own broth, and you should consider following their example. Homemade stock is free of additives, can be made with no added salt, and costs less to make than commercial products. Make a big batch, freeze it in 1- and 2-cup containers, and you'll be well-stocked (pardon the pun) for a long time.

Buying Broth

If, instead, you use canned broth, bouillon cubes, or a concentrate, choose a superior product. Read the label carefully, to make sure the product does not contain hydrogenated oil, MSG, and other additives you may not welcome. Be sure to compare samples of several products (in diluted form) before settling on a favorite; some may taste mainly of salt, while others will have a full-bodied flavor much closer to homemade broth.

All things being equal, a high-quality concentrate is, I think, the most convenient for single-portion cooking. The paste can be spooned from the jar and diluted with hot water to make the quantity needed, and it will keep indefinitely in the refrigerator. More than Gourmet is one brand of flavorful veal, chicken and vegetable bases sold in specialty food stores or by mail order (800/860-9385). I've also used a line of bases called More than Bouillon, available in some supermarkets.

Improvising

Use homemade or purchased bases in recipes or improvise your own soups by adding pastine (soup pasta), rice, slivered vegetables, leftover cubed meat, or other ingredients.

This versatile meat broth can be used in any recipe calling for chicken or beef broth. The old-fashioned stewing chicken has vanished from supermarkets and butcher shops, and chicken necks and backs can be hard to find, too. Fortunately, broth can be made successfully with chicken or turkey wings, which are sold separately in most supermarkets. If you don't spot soup bones in the meat department, ask a butcher for them.

All-Purpose Meat Broth

Makes 3 quarts   Prep: 15 minutes Cook: 2 hours

2 1/2 pounds chicken or turkey wings

2 cracked veal or beef bones

2 carrots, trimmed and cut into chunks

1 celery stalk, trimmed and cut into chunks

1 medium onion, quartered

1 or 2 bay leaves

1/2 teaspoon peppercorns

1 Rinse the chicken or turkey wings and lay them in the bottom of a large saucepan or stockpot. Add the veal bones, carrots, celery, onion, bay leaves, and peppercorns, and cover with water. Bring to a boil, reduce the heat to medium, and skim until no more scum rises to the top.

2 Reduce the heat to low and simmer the broth, partly covered, about 2 hours. Allow the broth to cool slightly, and pour through a fine-mesh strainer; refrigerate.

3 Spoon congealed fat off the top of the chilled broth. Return the amount that you expect to use within a week to the refrigerator and freeze the rest in 1- or 2-cup plastic containers.

Cook's Note

The omission of salt is deliberate. Leaving out the salt frees you to use the broth as an ingredient in any recipe, seasoning as appropriate.

PASTA & OTHER NOODLES

Pasta is my favorite fallback meal. Peering into my pantry at its most pitiful, I can usually find some spaghetti and the makings of a sauce.

Even when there are other choices, though, a steaming bowl of pasta or other noodles is often what I most want. Who could tire of a food capable of so many different incarnations?

The recipes I call "comfort pasta" are just one step beyond plain, but they are the ones I make most often. My daughter, Mary, feels the same way—after a hard day of schoolwork and sports, she often makes herself a bowlful of spaghetti the minute she walks in the door.

In a good restaurant, each portion of pasta is mixed with its sauce in a small sauté pan, over a burner. At home, too, "skillet sauces" are great. No need to dirty another container, and the sauce and pasta stay warm while you toss them.

"Bowl-ready" sauces are prepared and held at room temperature, to be mixed with freshly cooked pasta or noodles.

Many sauces are easy to make one portion at a time. But tomato-based sauces and pesto are another matter. They are so nice to have on hand that you may as well make a batch and save some for the freezer.

Pasta Primer

Portion Size

Two ounces is the usual portion size listed on packages, and that may be the right amount if pasta is a first course. But most of these recipes call for three ounces, based on my hunch that the typical single-portion cook plans to eat pasta as a main dish. Hearty eaters—and I am one—can easily finish off four ounces when pasta is the meal, so add the extra ounce if you feel so inclined.

Storage and Measuring

Dried pasta usually comes in a one-pound package—far too much for a single serving. After opening a bag of short pasta, such as macaroni, seal the bag tightly with a plastic clip or tie, or transfer the contents to a plastic container with a lid. You can weigh your portion or, if you like, measure it—a three-ounce serving consists of approximately one cup of short dried pasta.

I like to store spaghetti and other long pasta in a tall glass container made for that purpose. To simplify portioning, divide a pound of spaghetti into four to eight equal portions, securing each one with a plastic tie or rubber band. Or, find a trick for measuring a portion of long pasta. I know one solo cook who holds a bundle of angel hair pasta tightly in an upright position; if it fits onto a dime, it's just the right amount for her.

Fresh egg pasta, whether stuffed or not, should be refrigerated and eaten within a few days; the same is true of fresh Asian noodles. If using frozen stuffed pasta, remove only as much as needed from the freezer; rather than thawing it, drop the pasta directly into boiling water.

Water and Salt

Italians say to use enough water for the pasta to "swim," but you don't need to drown it. Six cups of cold water is plenty for a single serving. For this quantity, add half a tablespoon of salt. Don't be tempted to leave it out! The salt is needed to season the pasta properly—and most of it drains off with the water.

Cooking

After bringing the water to a boil, add the pasta all at once, pressing spaghetti and other long pasta with a wooden spoon to submerge it. Stir thoroughly to separate the strands or pieces, and boil the pasta to the al dente stage—tender but still slightly firm to the bite. The required time ranges from two or three minutes, for some fresh pasta, to twelve minutes for some dried pastas. The only way to tell for sure is to trap a piece with a slotted spoon or fork and taste it.

Draining

Don't overdo the draining. You may want to add a little of the starchy pasta water to the sauce. This can be accomplished by draining the pasta quickly in a colander and, without waiting for every bit of the water to go through, turning it into the sauce. Because it's a little easier to scoop out a quarter cup of the water before draining, that's the procedure followed in these recipes.

Saucing

Next, the pasta joins the sauce, in a warm skillet or bowl. Mix the two thoroughly, and add the reserved water if needed to give a good consistency. Grate cheese over the pasta when you sit down to eat.

Reheating

Cooking only as much pasta as you plan to eat at one sitting is ideal. But life is imperfect, and we all end up with leftovers sometimes. The easiest way to reheat pasta is to microwave it at half speed for two or three minutes, opening the door at 30-second intervals to stir.

I think the texture is better, however, when the leftover pasta is reheated in a sauté pan, over medium heat. Stir often and add a little water or broth if it seems too dry. Leftover pasta can also be steamed.

Pasta Glossary

There are dozens of varieties of pasta and noodles, and hundreds of shapes. Here are some of the most popular.

name	description
capellini	"angel's hair," consists of fine threads
cavatelli	finger-shaped pasta stuffed with cheese
egg noodles	often sold in loosely tangled balls, in a variety of widths; used in European and Asian recipes
farfalle	"butterflies," also called "bow ties"
fettuccine	egg pasta cut into flat, narrow strips
fusilli	spirals that are ideal for pasta salad or a tomato-based sauce
orecchiette	"little ears," great sauce catchers
pastine	all-purpose term for various tiny shapes suitable for simmering in broth
penne	short "quills," with or without ridges
rice noodles	round or flat strands from China or Southeast Asia
soba	Japanese buckwheat noodles, served hot or cold
somen	very fine, white wheat noodles from Japan
spaghetti	Italy's famous "little string" pasta (spaghettini are even skinnier)
tortellini	stuffed pasta dumplings, fresh or frozen; the dried kind are only for soups
vermicelli	"little worms," an uglier name for capellini; can stand in for Asian wheat noodles

When you're tired and starving, plain (or practically plain) pasta is just the thing.

Spaghetti with Butter and Cheese

Makes 1 serving   Prep: 5 minutes   Cook: 12 minutes

Salt
3 ounces spaghetti
1 1/2 tablespoons butter
1 1/2 tablespoons freshly grated Parmesan

1 Over high heat, bring 6 cups of water and 1/2 tablespoon of salt to a boil in a medium-size saucepan. Add the spaghetti and stir gently to immerse and separate the strands.

2 Meanwhile, melt the butter over low heat in a skillet large enough to hold the spaghetti.

3 After 10 minutes, when the spaghetti is almost done, remove the pan with the butter from the heat and mix in the Parmesan. Drain the cooked spaghetti, turn it into the sauce and mix well.

variations

• Add 1 cup of steamed or stir-fried vegetables (fresh or frozen) to the pasta.

• Substitute 4 ounces (about 1 cup) of frozen ravioli, cavatelli, or tortellini for the spaghetti.

• Brown the butter, taking care not to let it burn. Remove from the heat and stir in a little finely chopped garlic and dried or fresh sage before adding the pasta.

Spaghetti with Garlic and Oil

Makes 1 serving   Prep: 5 minutes   Cook: 12 minutes

variation

Spaghetti with Garlic and Shrimp: Sauté 1/2 cup small, shelled shrimp in the oil before adding the garlic; or, add 1/2 cup cooked shrimp to the final mixture.

Salt

3 ounces spaghetti

1 1/2 to 2 tablespoons extra-virgin olive oil

1 small, finely chopped garlic clove

1 tablespoon finely chopped fresh parsley

Dash of red pepper flakes

1 Over high heat, bring 6 cups of water and 1/2 tablespoon of salt to a boil in a medium-size saucepan. Add the spaghetti and stir gently to immerse and separate the strands.

2 While the spaghetti cooks, heat the oil and garlic in a skillet or sauté pan large enough to hold the pasta. When the garlic bits turn golden (watch to prevent burning), remove from the heat.

3 When the spaghetti is al dente, drain and turn it into the pan with the garlic sauce. Add the parsley and red pepper flakes, and mix well.

When I asked my friend Alice Gottlieb how to make egg noodles and cabbage, a dish I had heard of but never eaten, she said, "It's comfort food—there's not really a recipe."

Eventually, Alice relented and told me what to do, but she had a point. Once you've made this satisfying and extremely easy meal, you'll never need the recipe again, as long as you remember one rule: The amount of cabbage should be roughly equal in volume to the amount of egg noodles.

Egg Noodles and Cabbage

Makes 1 serving Prep: 10 minutes Cook: 15 minutes

2 tablespoons butter
2 cups shredded cabbage (about 2 cups) (see Note)
Salt and freshly ground black pepper to taste
3 ounces broad egg noodles

1 Melt the butter over medium heat in a skillet large enough to hold the cabbage and noodles. Cook the cabbage, stirring occasionally, until the shreds soften and brown around the edges; reduce the heat if the cabbage seems in danger of burning. Season with salt and pepper.

2 Meanwhile, bring 6 cups water and 1/2 tablespoon salt to a boil in a medium-size saucepan. Add the noodles, stirring gently to separate them, and cook until al dente, about 7 minutes. Drain and mix the noodles with the cabbage.

Cook's Note

What to do with the rest of that cabbage head? Cabbage is a vegetable that microwaves beautifully. Just cut off a wedge, trimming away most of the core, and put it into a microwaveable dish, along with a little chicken stock or water and a bit of butter. Season with celery salt and freshly ground black pepper, or kosher salt and caraway seeds, cover and microwave at full power until fork tender. If you toss a piece of kielbasa or a slice of ham into the dish, that can be dinner.

Hair stylists are a great source of recipes, and Karyn Palombo is no exception. She loves to cook but can't linger in the kitchen. To make time for daily gym workouts and friends, she invents sauces that are ready when the pasta is cooked.

Clam and Radicchio Sauce (for short pasta)

Makes 1 serving   Prep: 10 minutes   Cook: 12 minutes

Salt

1 teaspoon extra-virgin olive oil

1/2 teaspoon finely chopped garlic

1 or 2 diced plum tomatoes

1/2 cup shredded radicchio

1/2 cup chicken broth

3 ounces farfalle or other short pasta

1/2 cup whole drained clams (half a 10-ounce can)

1 Bring 6 cups of water and 1/2 tablespoon of salt to a boil in a medium-size saucepan. Meanwhile, heat the olive oil in a skillet large enough to hold the cooked pasta. Cook the garlic, tomatoes, and radicchio over medium heat until they soften, about 10 minutes. Stir in the chicken broth and simmer a few minutes longer.

2 Drop the pasta into the boiling water, stir to separate the pieces, and cook until al dente. Drain, and mix the pasta and clams into the tomato mixture.

Cook's Note

Use leftover clams within a day or two as an addition to vegetable soup, a tomato-based sauce for pasta, or in Spaghetti with Garlic and Oil (page 49).

Cooking on Two Continents

Spending most of each year in Italy is part of Richard Goldthwaite's enviable routine as a scholar of Renaissance economic history. That is the right place, as well, to indulge his love of Italian food, for any needed ingredient is just "two steps away"—as the Italian phrase goes—from his apartment in the center of Florence.

In Baltimore, where Richard teaches and writes the rest of the time, ingredients for Italian cooking are not as easy to come by, but he is resourceful enough to manage. Most dinners are all-in-one dishes, prepared and eaten while watching an hour-long news show on television.

In both cities, Richard cooks a mean minestrone, fortified with his homemade broth and beans. He knows how to cook cannellini beans with Italian sausage or roast a Rock Cornish hen with root vegetables. And he's likely to eat pasta several times a week. "When I was a student, I ate *pasta al burro* almost every day," he remembers. Though he still enjoys that simplest of pasta sauces, butter and cheese, his repertoire now includes orecchiette with broccoli and garlic ("heavy on the broccoli"), spaghetti with an uncooked tomato sauce, and spaghetti alla carbonara.

Broccoli and Garlic Sauce (for short pasta)

Makes 1 serving   Prep: 10 minutes   Cook: 12 minutes

1 medium broccoli stalk or several florets (about 2 cups, cut)
Salt
3 ounces orecchiette, penne or cavatelli (about 1 cup)
2 tablespoons extra-virgin olive oil
1 peeled garlic clove
1 tablespoon freshly grated Parmesan
Dash of red pepper flakes (optional)

1 Cut the broccoli stalk or florets into pieces about 1 inch long. Combine with 1/4 cup water in a microwaveable container; cover and microwave until the broccoli is barely cooked through, about 2 minutes (alternatively, steam the broccoli on top of the stove); drain.

2 Bring 6 cups of water and 1/2 tablespoon of salt to a boil in a medium-size saucepan. Cook the pasta until al dente.

3 Meanwhile, heat the oil on a medium setting in a skillet large enough to hold the pasta. Cook the garlic until golden brown on two sides (don't let it burn!), then remove it. Stir in the broccoli. Season with salt, and, when the broccoli pieces are heated through, reduce the heat to low.

4 Drain the pasta, reserving 1/4 cup water, and mix it with the broccoli. Add the pasta water if needed to thin the sauce. Top with Parmesan and red pepper flakes (if using).

variations

Broccoli Rabe Sauce: In place of broccoli, use an equivalent amount of broccoli rabe, proceeding in the same way.

Broccoli and Sausage Sauce: Add 2 ounces cooked sweet or hot Italian sausage chunks.

Low-Fat Broccoli Sauce: Substitute chicken stock for all or part of the olive oil, and add a squeeze of lemon juice just before eating.

I don't want creamy foods often, but when I do, this luxurious sauce satisfies the yen.

Creamy Seafood Sauce (for short pasta)

Makes 1 serving   Prep: 15 minutes   Cook: 12 minutes

Salt
1 teaspoon butter
1 tablespoon finely chopped shallot
3 tablespoons heavy cream
3 ounces farfalle or other short pasta
6 to 8 shrimp or scallops, or a combination
Torn tarragon leaves (optional)
Freshly ground white or black pepper

1 Bring 6 cups of water and 1/2 tablespoon of salt to a boil in a medium-size saucepan. Meanwhile, melt the butter in a skillet large enough to hold the cooked pasta. Add the shallot and cream, cover, and cook over low heat.

2 Stir the pasta into the boiling water. After 10 minutes, when the pasta is almost done, add the shrimp or scallops and a few tarragon leaves to the cream sauce. Season with salt and white or black pepper. Stir, cover, and cook until the shrimp turn pink.

3 Drain the cooked pasta (reserving 1/4 cup water), and stir the pasta into the shrimp sauce. Add pasta water if necessary to thin the sauce.

A thin skin and a sweet smell are clues, but the only sure way to judge a tomato is to bite into one. When the verdict is thumbs up, make this uncooked sauce that tastes like the essence of summer.

Fresh Tomato Sauce (for long pasta)

**Makes 1 serving   Prep: 10 minutes, plus marinating time
Cook (the pasta): 12 minutes**

1 large, vine-ripened tomato

4 medium basil leaves

1 1/2 tablespoons extra-virgin olive oil

1 small, finely chopped garlic clove

Freshly ground black pepper

Salt

3 ounces spaghetti or capellini

1 Using a sharp knife, strip away the skin of the tomato and cut out the stem end. Chop the tomato flesh roughly, saving as much liquid as possible, and transfer to a bowl large enough to hold the pasta and sauce.

2 Tear up the basil leaves and drop into the bowl, along with the olive oil, garlic, and a sprinkle of pepper. Cover the mixture and allow to marinate at room temperature 1 to 4 hours (refrigeration would diminish the flavor). Taste and season as needed with salt.

3 Bring 6 cups of water and 1/2 tablespoon of salt to a boil in a medium-size saucepan. Add the spaghetti or capellini, pressing with a wooden spoon to submerge it and stirring to separate the strands. Cook until al dente. Drain the pasta and mix gently with the tomato sauce.

Carbonara
(for long pasta)

Makes 1 serving   Prep: 10 minutes   Cook: 12 minutes

2 teaspoons butter

2 tablespoons finely chopped shallot or onion

1 slice pancetta, cut into small squares (see Note)

1 tablespoon vermouth or white wine

Salt

3 to 4 ounces spaghetti or linguine

1 egg yolk

1 tablespoon chopped fresh parsley

1 tablespoon freshly grated Parmesan

1 Combine the butter, shallot, and pancetta in a small skillet, over medium heat, and cook until the shallot is tender. Add the vermouth, and stir and cook until it has almost evaporated. Reduce heat to warm.

2 Bring 6 cups of water and 1/2 tablespoon of salt to a boil. Add the spaghetti, stirring to submerge and separate the strands.

3 While the pasta cooks, beat the egg yolk in a bowl large enough to hold the sauce and pasta, and mix in the parsley and Parmesan.

4 When the pasta is al dente, drain and immediately turn it into the bowl, lifting and turning the strands until all are coated; the heat of the pasta will cook the egg. Mix in the shallot-pancetta mixture.

Cook's Notes

● Look for pancetta (unsmoked Italian bacon) in the deli department of your supermarket or a specialty food store. If you cannot find it, substitute regular American bacon (drain off fat after cooking); the flavor is different but the sauce will taste good.

● In a well-made carbonara, the egg "cooks" just enough to coat the pasta properly. If the egg yolk is undercooked, the strands will feel slimy. Warming the bowl can be helpful, but watch out!—if it's too hot, the egg will separate into hardboiled bits.

Calvin Trillin once proposed that spaghetti alla carbonara be adopted as the national Thanksgiving meal. That may be going too far, but for the single-portion cook, a carbonara feast has considerably more appeal than roasting a turkey.

Spicy Peanut Sauce
(for long noodles)

Makes 1 serving   Prep: 10 minutes   Cook: 5 to 10 minutes

1 tablespoon peanut butter

2 teaspoons reduced-salt soy sauce

1 tablespoon unseasoned rice vinegar

1/4 teaspoon sugar

Dash of hot chile oil

3 ounces Asian wheat noodles, such as somen or udon, or linguine

1 Combine the peanut butter, soy sauce, rice vinegar, sugar, and hot chile oil in a bowl large enough to hold the cooked noodles. Whisk until the ingredients are well blended.

2 Meanwhile, bring 6 cups of water to a boil. Cook the Asian noodles until they are soft but not mushy, about 5 minutes (linguine will take about 10 minutes). Drain the noodles and cool under running water. Toss the noodles with the sauce.

This versatile tomato-based sauce is nice to have on hand, for pizza as well as pasta. Make sure that tomatoes, the main ingredient, are top quality. I prefer canned tomatoes imported from Italy (if you spot "San Marzano" on the label, that's good). You can also make a fresh-tasting sauce with pureed tomatoes in aseptic packaging (another Italian import, Pomì, is a good brand).

Basic Tomato Sauce

Makes about 2 quarts   Prep: 15 minutes   Cook: 1 hour

2 tablespoons extra-virgin olive oil

1 medium onion, chopped

2 finely chopped garlic cloves

1 finely chopped celery stalk

2 large (28-ounce) cans pureed or whole tomatoes

2 tablespoons tomato paste (from a tube)

1 teaspoon dried basil or oregano

1/4 teaspoon freshly ground black pepper

Salt if needed

1 In a large saucepan, heat the oil over medium heat, and cook the onion, garlic, and celery, covered, until tender but not browned.

2 Add the pureed tomatoes to the mixture. (If you are using whole tomatoes, drain the tomato juices into the pan, holding back the tomatoes with a spoon or spatula; crush the tomatoes with your fingers, letting the pulp fall into the pan.) Stir in the tomato paste, basil, and pepper.

3 Raise the heat to medium high and bring the mixture almost to a boil. Reduce the heat to low, cover the pan to prevent splattering, and simmer about an hour. Taste and add salt if any is needed.

4 Transfer the cooled sauce to microwave-safe containers, each holding 1 cup (2 servings). Seal, label, and freeze.

variations

Tomato-Pancetta Sauce: Cut a slice of pancetta (unsmoked Italian bacon) or regular American bacon into small squares, and lightly brown it. Drain off fat, add the olive oil, and continue with the recipe.

Tomato-Mushroom Sauce: Cover 1/2 ounce dried porcini or other dried mushrooms with warm water and soak at least 15 minutes. Lift the mushrooms from the water, rinse, chop, and sauté with the onions and other vegetables. After adding the tomatoes, hold a strainer lined with a paper towel or coffee filter over the saucepan and pour the mushroom water through it and into the sauce.

Buying a Decent Red Sauce

You are likely to find a dozen brands of tomato-based pasta sauce in your supermarket. A few may have a long-cooked, unpleasant taste, but most fall into the middle range—acceptable, but bland. With luck, though, you may find one with the aroma and taste of a good homemade sauce. My first choice is Rao's Homemade. If you can't find that, keep tasting until you find a worthy alternative.

You can buy tomato-based sauces containing extra ingredients such as roasted garlic or mushrooms, but only rarely do the flavors of the additional ingredients come through in a pronounced way. I prefer to buy a plain tomato-based sauce and enhance it at home.

Tomato Sauces with Something Extra

Whether you make your own tomato-based sauce or buy a good ready-made brand, adding an extra ingredient or two can make it taste more interesting. Survey your pantry or refrigerator for inspiration, or try these sauces, all proportioned for a 3-ounce pasta serving.

Tuna
(for spaghetti)

Brown 1 crushed garlic clove in 1 teaspoon of extra-virgin olive oil; remove the garlic clove, stir in 1/2 cup tomato-based sauce, and heat; just before eating, mix in 2 or 3 imported black olives, pitted and cut into slivers, 5 rinsed capers, and 1 ounce of drained tuna; stir in the cooked pasta.

Mushroom-Onion
(for short pasta)

Sauté 1/2 cup chopped mushrooms with 1/4 cup finely chopped onion or shallot in 1 tablespoon extra-virgin olive oil; stir in 1/2 cup tomato-based sauce and heat; stir in the cooked pasta.

Rapid Ragu
(for short pasta)

Sauté 2 ounces ground beef, turkey, or Italian-style sausage with 1/4 cup finely chopped onion or shallot; drain grease; stir in 1/2 cup tomato-based sauce and simmer 15 minutes, adding water as necessary to thin the sauce; mix in the cooked pasta and top with freshly grated Parmesan.

Pasta e Fagioli
(for short pasta)

In a microwave or on a burner, heat 1/2 cup tomato-based sauce with 1 cup drained white beans; mix in the cooked pasta and 1 tablespoon chopped fresh parsley.

Pesto is another great "for the freezer" sauce.

Pesto

Makes 1 cup   Prep: 20 minutes

2 cups fresh basil leaves, torn if large
1/2 cup extra-virgin olive oil
2 tablespoons pine nuts, pecans, or walnuts
2 lightly crushed garlic cloves
1 teaspoon salt
1 tablespoon freshly grated Parmesan (per portion)

1 Combine the basil, olive oil, pine nuts, garlic, and salt in a blender or food processor. Blend at high speed, stopping once or twice to scrape down the sides, until the ingredients are pureed.

2 Spoon the pesto into ice cube trays; transfer the frozen pesto cubes to recloseable plastic bags. For a single serving, thaw 1 cube (equal to 2 tablespoons). Or, you can spoon the pesto into microwave-safe containers, each holding 1/4 cup (2 portions); seal, label, and freeze.

3 When ready to use, thaw the pesto in the refrigerator, the microwave, or partly submerged in warm water. Blend 1 tablespoon of Parmesan per portion into the pesto.

STOVETOP COOKING

For those of us who like to feel in control of our dinner, if not our destiny, stovetop cooking is the answer. I can flash-cook my meal, or let it simmer at a leisurely pace. Best of all, it's right there for prodding or tasting—no need to open the oven or microwave door.

In this chapter, you'll find appetizing stovetop methods for preparing poultry, meat, and seafood. Soups, pastas, and vegetarian main dishes cooked on top of the stove are covered elsewhere in *Serves One*.

Chops and fillets are God's gift to the solo cook. Instead of coping with a roast, you can buy a steak or a chicken fillet just the right size for dinner. Another blessing: These small, tender cuts taste best when sautéed quickly on top of your stove, with a few simple seasonings.

Stir-frying is famous, and justly so, for its speed. By improvising or following one of these recipes, you can make a hot, flavorful meal in minutes. If you own a wok, use it. Otherwise, a medium-size skillet will work fine.

Steaming is equally rapid. Bring a little water or broth to a simmer, cover the pot with your dinner inside, and, by the time you've set your table or tray, it will be ready.

Stews are a little pokier, but worth the wait, especially if you make enough for two or more meals.

The ideal companions for these chops are Greek Salad (page 20) and Rice Pilaf (page 101).

Pan-Fried Lamb Chops

Makes 1 serving   Prep: 5 minutes   Cook: 5 minutes

8 ounces lamb chops (1 or 2 loin chops; 3 or 4 rib chops)
1 peeled and crushed garlic clove
Salt and freshly ground black pepper to taste
1 teaspoon vegetable oil
1 lemon wedge

1 Half an hour before you plan to eat, trim all but a thin border of fat from the lamb chops and blot them with a paper towel. Rub both sides with garlic, and sprinkle with salt and pepper.

2 Heat the vegetable oil over high heat in a small, heavy skillet or a ridged grill pan (preferably nonstick). Brown the chops on both sides; this will take no longer than a minute. Lower the heat to medium and cook four minutes longer, for medium-rare chops (deduct a minute for rare chops; add a minute or two for well done).

3 Squeeze the lemon over the chops just before eating.

Cook's Note

The method described here works well for chops up to 1 inch thick. If yours are thicker, stir in a little wine, water, or broth after the initial searing of the chops, cover, and cook to the desired degree of doneness.

Peppered Steak

Makes 1 generous serving   Prep: 5 minutes   Cook: 10 minutes

1 boneless 8-ounce beef steak (see Note)

2 teaspoons black peppercorns

Up to 1 teaspoon vegetable oil

Salt to taste

1/4 cup red wine

1 About half an hour before you plan to eat, trim all but a thin border of fat from the steak. Using a mortar and pestle, crush the peppercorns until most are broken into several pieces (alternatively, use a potato masher or meat pounder and a sturdy stainless-steel bowl). Blot the steak with a paper towel and coat both sides with the peppercorns.

2 When the steak has warmed nearly to room temperature, brush a small, heavy skillet or ridged grill pan with the oil (if it has a nonstick surface, you will need very little). Heat the pan until very hot. Lay the steak in the pan and reduce the heat to medium high. After browning both sides of the steak, continue to cook a total of 6 minutes for medium-rare (see Note). Remove the steak from the pan, sprinkle with salt, and allow to rest several minutes.

3 Meanwhile, pour the red wine into the skillet and, stirring to loosen any meat bits, cook a minute or two until the liquid thickens slightly. Pour the sauce over the steak.

Cook's Notes

● Choose a tender, well-marbled cut such as a shell steak, porterhouse, rib-eye, or filet mignon.

● Deduct a minute from the cooking for rare steak and add a minute for well done. Timing the steak is a helpful but, to be honest, not a foolproof way to achieve the desired doneness. As any restaurant grill cook knows, pressing the steak with a thumb provides an extra clue. If the steak feels soft, it's rare; a steak that yields slightly but still springs back is medium rare; if it feels firm, it's well done.

Most seasonings interfere with the fine qualities of a good steak. But I make an exception for generous quantities of coarsely ground black pepper, which bring out every bit of beefy flavor.

Homemade chicken fingers or nuggets are easy to make and are far superior to fast-food or frozen products. You can substitute a light, crisp coating for the heavy, armorlike casing found on the commercial tidbits. Pan-frying chicken in a polyunsaturated oil, rather than deep-frying in partially hydrogenated oil, is, from a health standpoint, definitely better. And, the homemade fingers taste a whole lot better.

Chicken Fingers

Makes 1 serving   Prep: 10 minutes   Cook: 6 minutes

1 skinless, boneless chicken breast half

2 tablespoons milk

1/4 cup dry, seasoned (Italian or all-purpose) bread crumbs

1 tablespoon vegetable oil (such as canola)

1 lemon wedge

1 Trim any visible fat from the chicken breast. Lightly pound it to a uniform thickness, and cut into "fingers" about 1/2 inch by 2 inches. In a small bowl, combine the chicken with the milk, turning the pieces until all are moistened.

2 When you are ready to cook, coat the pieces with the bread crumbs. Heat the oil over medium-high heat in a medium-size skillet (preferably nonstick). Using tongs or a spatula, space out the chicken fingers in the skillet and reduce the heat to medium. Cook the fingers until they are browned on both sides and the inside is cooked through, about 6 minutes.

3 Drain the fingers on a paper towel, and add a squeeze of lemon.

variations

Fish Fingers: Instead of chicken, use a flounder fillet (or any other thin, mild-flavored fish). Proceed as in the main recipe. Sprinkle the cooked fish with malt vinegar, or rice vinegar, or lemon juice.

Sesame-Crusted Chicken: Dip a lightly pounded chicken breast half in 1/4 cup milk and then in a mixture of 1/4 cup flour, 1 teaspoon sesame seeds, and 1/4 teapoon grated lemon zest. Proceed as in the main recipe.

Lemon Chicken

**Makes 2 servings   Prep: 15 minutes, plus marinating time
Cook: 8 minutes**

3/4 pound boneless, skinless chicken breast (2 halves)

1/2 teaspoon salt

1/4 teaspoon plus 1 tablespoon sugar

Dash of black or white pepper

2 teaspoons plus 1 teaspoon cornstarch

2 teaspoons ginger wine (see Note)

1 tablespoon lemon juice

1 to 2 tablespoons ketchup

1 to 2 teaspoons reduced-sodium soy sauce

1 Trim any visible fat from the chicken. Using a mallet, flatten the chicken breast halves to an even thickness.

2 Combine the salt, 1/4 teaspoon sugar, black pepper, 2 teaspoons cornstarch, and ginger wine in a 1-quart recloseable plastic bag; massage the outside of the bag to mix the ingredients and dissolve the cornstarch. Place the fillets in the bag and, forcing out air, seal the bag. Turn the bag until the fillets are coated on all sides. Marinate, refrigerated, 1 to 24 hours.

3 Combine the remaining tablespoon of sugar, remaining teaspoon of cornstarch, lemon juice, ketchup, and soy sauce with 1/4 cup water in a small skillet. Stirring occasionally, bring the mixture to a simmer. Add the chicken with its marinade and, when the liquid begins to bubble again, lower the heat to medium low and cover the skillet.

4 Cook the chicken, turning once, until tender, about 5 to 8 minutes; check often and add more water if the chicken seems too dry.

Cook's Note

To make ginger wine, place any amount of peeled, thinly sliced gingerroot in a clean glass jar with a tight-fitting lid. Cover with dry sherry. Refrigerate and use as needed to season meat, poultry, and vegetable stir-fries. Add more sherry when the ginger wine runs low; chilled, it will keep several weeks.

Who would guess that this golden-brown chicken breast was cooked with no added fat? Norma Chang, a cooking teacher in Wappinger Falls, New York, adapted this recipe from one in her self-published cookbook, *Wokking Your Way to Low-Fat Cooking*.

Norma recommends making a double portion because "leftovers taste better the next day." I like to eat the chicken the first night with stir-fried vegetables and rice, and slice the remainder the following day to pile on a sandwich or on top of a salad.

Joan Surnamer is an exception to the "rule" that New Yorkers never eat in. After retiring from an executive position with Macy's, this skilled cook acquired the pleasant habit of buying ingredients for her single-portion dinners at the Union Square Greenmarket.

Joan's recipe is based on a dish she once ate in an Italian restaurant. "I tried a few times, and then one day I *got* it," she says. Be sure to eat this fish dinner with a slice of coarse, crusty bread, to catch the delicious juices.

Flounder with Tomatoes and Peppers

Makes 1 serving   Prep: 10 minutes   Cook: 15 minutes

2 teaspoons extra-virgin olive oil

1/3 cup finely chopped onion or shallot

1 small Italian frying pepper or other mild pepper, chopped (about 2/3 cup)

2 plum tomatoes, stemmed and chopped

1 to 2 teaspoons capers, rinsed

2 or 3 imported black olives, such as Kalamata or niçoise, pitted and slivered

1 sprig Italian parsley, chopped

1 or 2 flounder fillets or other thin, mild-flavored fish fillets (about 5 ounces)

Salt and freshly ground black pepper

1 Heat the olive oil over low heat in a small skillet (preferably nonstick). Cook the onion until it softens and turns translucent. Add the pepper and tomatoes; cover and simmer until the tomatoes release their juices, about 10 minutes.

2 Stir in the capers, olives, and parsley. Arrange the flounder fillet on the bed of vegetables, spooning some of the juices on top. Season the fish and vegetables with salt and pepper. Cover and simmer until the fish is cooked through, about 5 minutes.

Stir-Frying: A Good Idea, on Balance

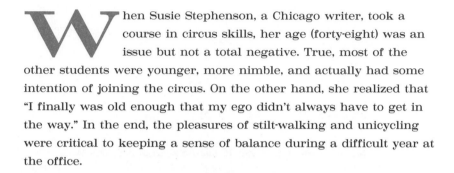

When Susie Stephenson, a Chicago writer, took a course in circus skills, her age (forty-eight) was an issue but not a total negative. True, most of the other students were younger, more nimble, and actually had some intention of joining the circus. On the other hand, she realized that "I finally was old enough that my ego didn't always have to get in the way." In the end, the pleasures of stilt-walking and unicycling were critical to keeping a sense of balance during a difficult year at the office.

The circus course was not out of character. Middle age also inspired Susie to earn an MBA, take up fly-fishing, and acquire a kayak for warm-weather paddling in Lake Michigan.

It takes a sense of adventure and good organization to live this way, and that's how Susie operates in the kitchen, too. She especially revels in the spontaneous but orderly process of stir frying. How dinner turns out depends on her energy level, mood, and kitchen supplies.

A typical free-form recipe from Susie is for refried rice:

• Heat a little oil in a wok and sauté chopped garlic and fresh ginger (keep it in the freezer to grate as you need it).

• Throw in cold brown rice and chopped up, cooked leftovers such as chicken, grilled tuna, veggies or scrambled eggs. If you don't have any of those, you can use frozen peas, corn, carrots or whatever you have on hand. Chopped red pepper adds color.

• Cook that until it's hot, throw in a little soy sauce, and when you think it's done, toss on some chopped scallions. If you've got a little sesame oil around, that's a tasty addition, too.

Machie Sakai, a freelance writer, enjoys making simple wok-cooked meals to eat with rice. She often doubles or triples this recipe, to trade with single friends in return for their specialties. Vary the meat and vegetables, but don't leave out the oyster sauce: It "gives a professional taste," in Machie's opinion.

Chicken, Tofu, and Watercress Stir-Fry

Makes 1 serving   Prep: 15 minutes   Cook: 5 minutes

2 teaspoons vegetable oil

1 boneless, skinless chicken thigh or breast half, cut into 1/2-inch cubes

3 ounces extra-firm or firm tofu, cut into 1/2-inch cubes (1/2 cup) (see Note)

2 tablespoons Chinese oyster sauce

1/4 cup water or broth

Half a bunch watercress (about 2 cups, loosely packed), cut into 2-inch lengths

1 Heat the oil over high heat in a medium-size wok or skillet. When it is very hot, cook the chicken and tofu cubes, stirring often to brown on all sides. Meanwhile, combine the oyster sauce with the water

2 Stir the liquid into the stir-fry and, when it is hot, add the watercress. Reduce the heat to low, cover the pan and cook a minute or two, until the chicken is cooked through and the mixture is hot.

Cook's Note

Tofu labeled "extra-firm" is best; because it has a lower water content, the cubes brown more readily and have a more pleasing texture. (For more tofu tips, see page 100.)

Chef Pamela White steams Maine's glorious shellfish by the bushel during high season at coastal inns. Each succulent serving takes just a few minutes to make and, using Pam's method, you can do the same thing at home.

To round out the meal, you need only French bread and a tossed green salad.

Shellfish Steamer

Makes 1 serving   Prep: 15 minutes   Cook: 5 minutes

10 farm-raised mussels

4 cherrystone (littleneck) clams

1 tablespoon finely chopped shallot or onion

1 small garlic clove, finely chopped

1 teaspoon butter, cut in bits

1 tablespoon chopped fresh parsley, chervil, or tarragon

1/2 cup dry white vermouth or white wine

1 Cover the mussels and clams with cold water. Remove them one at a time and scrub under cold running water to remove any grit or sand; with a paring knife, pull off any "beards" clinging to shells.

2 Choose a skillet or saucepan large enough to hold the shellfish in a single layer and deep enough to cover once they are inside. Place the clams and mussels in the pan. Scatter the shallot, garlic, butter, and parsley over the shellfish, and pour the vermouth over them. Cover the pan.

3 Over medium-high heat, steam the shellfish until they open, about 5 minutes (the mussels will open first); discard any that fail to open. Using tongs, transfer the shellfish to a large, shallow soup bowl (or, use a small serving bowl). Pour the broth over them (strain out the solid ingredients if you like).

This recipe for posole, the Mexican marriage of pork and hominy, omits the pigs' feet and cuts a few other culinary corners to produce a savory stew in less than an hour. You can eat some right away, but the posole will have a richer, more stew-like character after being reheated a day or two later.

Posole Presto

Makes 2 servings   Prep: 15 minutes   Cook: 40 minutes

1 dried chile (ancho, guajillo, New Mexico red, etc.) (see Note)

1 1/2 cups hominy (one 15-ounce can), drained and rinsed

1 boneless pork chop (4 to 5 ounces), trimmed and cut into 1/2-inch cubes

1/3 cup chopped onion

1/2 teaspoon salt

1 small zucchini, cut into 1/2-inch cubes

1 Bring about 4 cups of water to a boil in a kettle. Break the chile into several pieces, discarding the stem, veins, and seeds. Place the chile pieces in a small bowl and cover with some of the boiling water. Allow to stand 10 minutes, until soft; drain.

2 Place the chile pieces in a blender or food processor container with half of the hominy and 1 cup boiling water; puree until thick but somewhat chunky.

3 Combine the pork cubes, onion, and salt in a medium-size saucepan. Pour the hominy-chile blend over the pork mixture. Bring to a simmer, cover, and cook gently until the pork cubes are tender.

4 Stir the remaining hominy and the zucchini cubes into the stew, and add enough hot water to barely cover the ingredients. Cook, uncovered, over low heat until the zucchini is tender and the flavors blend.

Cook's Note

In the Southwest, dried chiles are readily available even in supermarkets. If you live elsewhere, ask a friend to mail some chiles, or look for them in specialty food markets.

73

A potful of this basic beef stew, made with mustard and beer in the Belgian style, is a wonderful asset. Single servings, stockpiled in your freezer, thaw and reheat beautifully, and can be served in several different ways.

Belgian Beef Stew

Makes about 6 cups   Prep: 20 minutes   Cook: 2 hours

2 1/2 pounds beef chuck or round

3/4 cup flour

1 teaspoon salt, plus more as needed

1/2 teaspoon freshly ground black pepper

1/4 vegetable oil, or more as needed

1 large onion, finely chopped

1 or 2 garlic cloves, finely chopped

2 bottles dark beer, plus enough water to make 4 cups

1/4 cup malt vinegar or cider vinegar

2 bay leaves

1/2 teaspoon thyme

1 tablespoon Dijon mustard

variation

Beef Stew with Red Wine: Substitute red wine and red wine vinegar for the beer and malt vinegar. Omit the flour and the coating process, and the mustard.

1 Trim fat and gristle from the beef and cut into 1-inch cubes. Combine the flour, salt, and pepper in a wide, shallow container such as a pie plate.

2 Heat half of the oil in a skillet over medium heat. Cook the onion until translucent. Add the garlic and cook another minute. Scrape the mixture into a saucepan large enough to hold all the stew ingredients.

3 Wipe out the skillet with a paper towel. Using your hands, coat the beef with the seasoned flour, patting the cubes so that excess flour falls away. Heat the remaining oil in the skillet over high heat and, when it is sizzling hot, space out the cubes in the pan so they do not touch (do in batches, adding more oil if necessary). Cook the cubes, turning them with tongs, until all are browned well on at least 2 sides. Transfer the beef cubes as they are done to the saucepan.

4 After moving the last of the cubes to the saucepan, reduce the heat under the skillet to medium and pour in the beer and water mixture, and the malt vinegar, stirring to loosen any bits stuck to the bottom. Stir in the bay leaves, thyme, and mustard, and bring to a boil. Pour the mixture over the beef cubes and add enough water to cover.

5 Heat the stew until it is nearly boiling, reduce the heat to low, and simmer until the beef cubes are tender. Taste and add more salt if necessary.

Cook's Notes

● The ingredients will be tender at the end of the cooking time. Like most stews, however, this will be thicker and have more flavor the next day.

● Refrigerate the stew or freeze some in 2-cup plastic containers or 1-quart recloseable plastic bags.

Single-Serving Suggestions

Plain Beef Stew: Simmer 1 1/2 cups of the stew until very thick. Serve plain with new potatoes or a baked potato, or on egg noodles.

Beef Stew with Root Vegetables: Peel root vegetables (turnips, potatoes, parsnips, and carrots, in any combination) and cut into chunks about the same size as the beef cubes, until you have 2 cups of vegetables. Mix with 1 1/2 cups of beef stew, adding more water if needed, and simmer until the vegetables are tender. (An even faster method is to steam or boil the vegetables separately before combining with the heated beef stew.)

Beef Stew with Mushrooms and Pearl Onions: To a serving of stew, add 3 trimmed and quartered white or exotic mushrooms and 1/2 cup peeled pearl onions (boil the onions for a minute or two to make removal of skins easier). Simmer until the vegetables are tender and spoon the stew over rice or noodles.

More Stovetop Meals

These one-pot meals prove that ease of preparation and delicious dining are quite compatible.

Sauerkraut and Sausage

Drain 1 1/2 cups precooked sauerkraut (plain or with caraway seeds).

In a small saucepan, combine the sauerkraut with 4 ounces of Polish kielbasa or another kind of cooked, cured sausage, cut into bite-size chunks. Add enough water, wine, or beer to barely cover the mixture.

Cook, covered, over medium-low heat until the sauerkraut and sausage are heated through. Eat with a grainy Dijon mustard and a green salad.

Steamed Shrimp Dinner

Cut a medium, thin-skinned potato into chunks and sprinkle with Old Bay Seasoning and salt. Steam over equal parts water and vinegar.

Meanwhile, cut an ear of corn into 3 or 4 pieces and rinse 8 to 12 large, unpeeled shrimp. When the potato is tender, add the corn pieces and shrimp to the steamer. Sprinkle with Old Bay Seasoning and salt, and steam until the corn is tender and the shrimp turn pink.

Peel the shrimp at the table, eating them and the vegetables as they are or dipping them into melted butter and lemon juice.

Breaded Liver with Sage

Dredge a 5-ounce piece of calf's liver in dry seasoned bread crumbs. Over medium heat, sauté several sage leaves in a little butter and olive oil until slightly crisp but not blackened; remove. In the same skillet, sauté the liver on both sides until the outside is crusty, but the interior is pink. Place the sage leaves on top of the liver, and sprinkle with lemon juice.

Creamed Turkey or Tuna (2 servings)

Melt 1 tablespoon butter in a small saucepan. Stir in 1 tablespoon flour and, over low heat, cook 2 to 3 minutes.

While continuing to stir, gradually add 1/2 cup milk. When the mixture has cooked to a smooth, medium-thick consistency, season with freshly ground white or black pepper and a dash of Worcestershire.

Stir in the drained contents of a 6-ounce can of tuna or 1 cup cooked turkey cubes, and cook until the mixture is heated through. Taste and add salt as necessary. Spoon over toast.

FROM OVEN & GRILL

A roast bird or baked meat loaf may sound like more food than a solo cook normally needs. But I have found that, with a little downsizing, such fare is more than feasible. An oven-cooked Rock Cornish hen is the right quantity for one or two meals, and a modestly sized meat loaf tastes just as good as a large one.

A foil-wrapped packet with the whole meal inside is another appealing option for solo cooks. In fact, you could cook and eat the meal without soiling a plate.

Grilling, another dry-heat method, is used for other recipes in this chapter. If you normally fire up your grill only for friends and family, reconsider. One solo cook I know has devised a pleasant routine that begins with starting her grill. While it heats, she prepares the meal and cleans up any kitchen mess. Then there's nothing to do but grill dinner and enjoy every bite.

Once the oven or grill is hot, you may as well cook the whole meal. With that goal in mind, some recipes are for all-in-one dishes, while others suggest side dishes to cook with the main course.

Sea bass or another thick fish fillet is browned on top of the stove in this recipe, based on an improvisation by my husband, Kent. In the same cast-iron pan, it slides into the oven for such a quick roasting that the onions still have a little crunch when you eat them.

A good side dish would be Roasted Vegetables (page 110) or Roasted Beets with Bitter Greens (page 23); cook the vegetables before the fish goes in.

Sea Bass with Capers

Makes 1 serving   Prep: 5 minutes   Cook: 15 minutes

One 6-ounce sea bass, grouper or cod fillet
1/2 small red onion, chopped
1 teaspoon capers, rinsed
2 teaspoons vegetable oil
Salt and freshly ground black pepper to taste
1/4 cup dry white vermouth or white wine

1 Preheat the oven to 425 degrees.

2 Pat the sea bass fillet dry with a paper towel. Mix together the onion and capers.

3 Over high heat, heat the vegetable oil in a small ovenproof skillet (preferably cast iron) until it is very hot. Place the fillet skin side down in the pan, and cook about 1 minute, until it browns. Using a spatula, turn the fillet and cook a minute or two on the other side.

4 Off the heat, season the fillet with salt and pepper, and spoon the onion-caper mixture on top (the skinless side). Pour the vermouth over the fish. Cook in the oven until the thickest part of the fillet looks opaque, about 10 minutes.

True to Her Roots

from her earliest years, Christina Erridge has adored the earthy flavors of root vegetables. Everyone in her English-born family feels the same way. It was only natural, then, that when Christina was a preschooler in California, and her class set out to make vegetable soup, she brought in a little bag of parsnips and turnips.

"I was sure everyone would love them. But the teacher sent the vegetables back home with me. She just didn't know what to do with them," Christina laments.

Traumatic as that experience was, Christina has stayed close to her roots. As a young public relations executive for Marriott International in Washington, D.C., she lives with three roommates, who often "do their own thing" when dinnertime rolls around. Christina's thing, quite often, is an oven-baked parsnip casserole or a roast surrounded by vegetables.

The following day she might use leftovers to make that English oddity known as "bubble and squeak." Christina explains how: "You take well-cooked vegetables from your Sunday dinner—maybe some mashed potatoes, carrots and brussels sprouts—and mix them with a little egg, pepper, salt and maybe milk. Then you fry the patty and eat it with green tomato chutney or A-1 sauce. It's a simple and comforting thing."

Rock Cornish Hen with Root Vegetables

Makes 1 or 2 servings   Prep: 15 minutes   Cook: 30 minutes

Thanks to the alchemy wrought by balsamic vinegar, olive oil, and rosemary, your hen will emerge from the oven golden-skinned and fragrant. The encircling root vegetables, nicely browned, finish the meal.

Cooking the small bird with the back facing up keeps the breast from drying out. To make 2 servings, cut the cooked hen in half, positioning the knife to one side of the backbone.

1 Rock Cornish hen or poussin (about 1 1/2 pounds)

1 large, crushed garlic clove

1 teaspoon balsamic vinegar

1 teaspoon plus 1 tablespoon extra-virgin olive oil

1 large sprig fresh rosemary or 1/2 teaspoon dried rosemary

Salt

1 small onion, peeled

1 medium carrot, peeled

1 medium russet potato, unpeeled, or 1 medium parsnip or turnip, peeled

Freshly ground black pepper

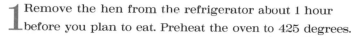

1 Remove the hen from the refrigerator about 1 hour before you plan to eat. Preheat the oven to 425 degrees.

2 Rinse the hen and pat the skin dry with a paper towel. Place it, breast side down, in a medium-size, ovenproof skillet (preferably cast iron) or small roasting pan. Disengage the legs at the joints and press down firmly on the back to flatten the hen.

3 Rub the skin with crushed garlic and insert what is left in the throat cavity. Rub first the balsamic vinegar and then the 1 teaspoon of olive oil onto the skin. Place half of the rosemary sprig in the cavity, together with a pinch of salt; rub the remaining leaves on the outside.

4 Quarter the onion and cut the other vegetables into fairly large chunks. Surround the chicken with the cut vegetables. Drizzle the remaining 1 tablespoon of olive oil over the vegetables, turning them until they are lightly coated. Sprinkle the vegetables with salt, and grind black pepper over the chicken and vegetables.

5 Place the skillet on a rack set in the middle of the oven. Roast 30 minutes, basting the bird and vegetables once or twice. Check to make sure the juices run clear (if not, return to the oven for a few minutes). Allow the hen to rest 10 minutes before cutting into it.

If you like to eat meat loaf hot the first day, but have enough left over for sandwiches, this mini meat loaf is for you (be sure to bake a russet or sweet potato alongside it). Or, you can make croquettes to cook one at a time.

Mini Meat Loaf

Makes 1 mini meat loaf or 4 croquettes Prep: 20 minutes
Cook: 30 minutes

1 strip of bacon or slice of pancetta (Italian unsmoked bacon), cut into small squares

1/3 cup finely chopped onion

1/3 cup finely chopped red or green pepper

1 teaspoon vegetable oil (if needed)

1 finely chopped garlic clove

1/2 pound ground beef (chuck or sirloin)

1/2 pound ground veal

1/3 cup tomato-based pasta sauce

1 egg

2/3 cup fresh bread crumbs

1/2 teaspoon salt

1/8 teaspoon freshly ground black pepper

2 teaspoons fresh, chopped sage or 1/8 teaspoon dried sage

1 Preheat the oven to 350 degrees.

2 Cook the bacon or pancetta, onion, and pepper in a small skillet, over medium heat, until the vegetables are tender and the bacon is lightly browned but not crisp; add the vegetable oil only if needed to keep the ingredients from burning. Stir in the garlic and cook another minute. Allow the mixture to cool.

3 Combine the ground beef, veal, pasta sauce, egg, bread crumbs, salt, pepper, and sage in a bowl. Add the bacon-onion mixture, and thoroughly mix the ingredients with your hands.

variation

Meat Loaf Croquettes: Divide the uncooked mixture into 4 parts, each weighing about 5 ounces, and form them into patties. Individually wrap the croquettes that you do not plan to eat immediately, label, and freeze.

To cook a croquette, heat a small skillet over a medium-high burner. Brown the croquette on both sides, reduce the heat to medium, and cook about 5 minutes longer; drain on a paper towel.

4 Form the mixture into a loaf shape, and place it on a small, foil-lined baking sheet with edges high enough to catch the fat given off by the meat loaf as it cooks. Bake about 30 minutes, until the outside is browned and the interior is cooked through (160 degrees on an instant-read thermometer).

Though ribs need time to cook, they don't require much work. Cheesy Potatoes and Pineapple Chunks (page 91), cooked with the ribs, are the side dishes of choice.

Oven-Barbecued Pork Ribs

Makes 1 generous serving Prep: 5 minutes   Cook: 1 1/4 hours

1 pound country-style or baby back pork ribs

1/4 cup hoisin sauce or barbecue sauce (see Note)

1 Preheat the oven to 350 degrees.

2 Place the pork ribs in a foil-lined roasting pan. Brush half of the hoisin or barbecue sauce over both sides of the ribs. Cover the pan with foil.

3 Cook the ribs until the meat is fairly tender when pierced with a fork, about 45 minutes. Pour off the fat, and brush on more of the sauce.

4 Raise the heat to 400 degrees and cook the ribs, uncovered, until they are dark brown and the meat is tender, about 30 minutes.

Cook's Notes

● To make the hoisin or barbecue sauce easier to spread, heat it about 15 seconds in the microwave at full power.

● For a more authentic barbecue flavor, cook the ribs on a moderately hot grill the last half hour, turning often.

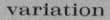

variation

Barbecued Chicken Thighs: Substitute 3 chicken thighs for the ribs. After applying the sauce, cook the chicken in a preheated 350-degree oven or on a moderately hot grill until the meat is tender and the skin is dark brown, about 40 minutes.

Ham and Potato Dinner

Makes 1 serving Prep: 10 minutes Cook: 15 minutes

3 ounces thick-cut ham (see Note)
1 small thin-skinned potato, peeled
1 small carrot, peeled
1/2 small onion
1/2 stalk celery
Salt and freshly ground black pepper to taste
2 tablespoons half-and-half or broth

If you were ever a Boy Scout or Girl Scout, this recipe may bring back memories of foil-wrapped dinners cooked in the hot ashes of a campfire.

1 Preheat the oven to 450 degrees.

2 Cut the ham into 1/2-inch cubes Cut the potato, carrot, onion, and celery into 1/8-inch slices.

3 Tear off a 12 by 18-inch piece of heavy-duty foil. Arrange the vegetable slices along the length of the less shiny side of the foil, leaving a 1-inch border on all sides. Season with salt (sparingly, because the ham contains salt) and pepper. Drizzle the half-and-half over the vegetables, and scatter the ham on top.

4 Draw together the long edges of foil and fold over several times, crimping tightly to prevent leakage but leaving room inside the packet for heat circulation; seal the ends in the same way.

5 Place the packet on a baking sheet and cook 15 minutes. Transfer the packet to a plate and wait 5 minutes before opening, to allow the meal to finish steaming.

Cook's Note

You can buy a thick-cut slice of baked ham at a deli counter or a small whole ham (about 1 1/2 pounds). Leftover ham can be sliced for sandwiches or cubed for a split pea soup.

More Foil-Wrapped Meals

Salmon-Potato Packet

On the 12 by 18-inch foil, arrange 6 ounces of salmon fillet and 1 small, thin-skinned potato cut into slices 1/8 inch thick. Rinse 3 pitted black imported olives (such as Kalamata) and 4 capers, and scatter on top. Season the salmon and potato with salt and either freshly ground black pepper or white pepper, and sprinkle on 1 tablespoon extra-virgin olive oil and 1 tablespoon dry white vermouth. Place 2 thin lemon slices on top. Follow the directions in the main recipe for sealing and baking.

Shrimp Succotash

Combine 6 shelled jumbo shrimp, 1/2 cup fresh or frozen corn, 1/2 cup thinly sliced zucchini, 1 chopped scallion and 1 diced plum tomato on the foil. Season with salt and either freshly ground black pepper or red pepper flakes, and drizzle with 1 1/2 teaspoons extra-virgin olive oil. Follow the directions in the main recipe for sealing and baking.

Improvising Foil-Wrapped Meals

Ingredients: Choose foods that will steam in about 15 minutes in a 450-degree oven. Boneless poultry, fish, and shellfish are good choices, as are most vegetables.

Prepping: Slice ingredients so that they will cook in roughly the same amount of time. Potato or carrot slices must be very thin, for example, while a faster-cooking vegetable such as celery can be cut into bigger pieces. The combined ingredients should weigh about 10 ounces. Otherwise, overcooking or undercooking could be a risk.

Seasonings: Experiment with adding fresh or dried herbs, vinegars, and a touch of olive oil, butter, cream, or broth.

Grill vegetables or corn (page 91) to go with the shrimp.

Skewered Shrimp

Makes 1 serving Prep: 5 minutes (plus marinating)
Grill: 5 minutes

1 finely chopped garlic clove

1 tablespoon extra-virgin olive oil

1 tablespoon lemon juice

Dash of red pepper flakes

4 jumbo shrimp

1 If you plan to use a bamboo skewer, soak it in water at least 10 minutes.

2 In a small bowl, whisk together the garlic, olive oil, lemon juice, and red pepper flakes. Turn the shrimp in the mixture until well coated. Push a metal or bamboo skewer through the shrimp, bending each one so that both tips are secured. Marinate 15 minutes to 1 hour.

3 On a hot grill, cook the shrimp 3 to 5 minutes, turning once, until they turn pink. Or, broil the shrimp on the uppermost rack of the oven.

variation

Microwaved Shrimp: Place the marinated shrimp (no skewer) in a microwaveable dish, cover with plastic wrap, and microwave at full power about 1 minute. Uncover and stir. Continue microwaving until the shrimp turn pink, about 30 seconds.

Grilled vegetables or an ear of corn (page 91) go well with the tuna steak.

Grilled Tuna Steak

**Makes 1 serving   Prep: 15 minutes, plus marinating time
Grill: 6 to 7 minutes**

2 teaspoons reduced-sodium soy sauce

1 teaspoon mirin (Japanese sweet rice wine)

1/2 teaspoon grated gingerroot

1/4 teaspoon finely chopped garlic

1 medium tuna steak (about 8 ounces)

1 sprig fresh cilantro (optional)

1 Combine the soy sauce, mirin, gingerroot, and garlic in a 1-quart recloseable plastic bag. Add the tuna steak, seal the bag and turn it over several times to coat with the mixture. Marinate 15 minutes to 2 hours.

2 On a hot grill, cook the tuna, turning once. For medium rare, grill about 6 minutes; for medium, about 7 minutes. Sprinkle fresh cilantro leaves, if using, on top of the steak.

Grilling brings out the rich flavor of a portobello mushroom and, as Jack Czarnecki points out in his *Portobello Cookbook*, a little soy enhances its earthy flavor. Eat the cap with knife and fork, or put it on a bun with any trimmings you like. Cheesy Potatoes, grilled alongside the portobello, are a good companion (page 91).

Grilled Portobello Cap

Makes 1 serving   Prep: 10 minutes   Cook: 6 minutes

1 medium portobello cap, about 4 inches across
1/2 teaspoon reduced-sodium soy sauce
1 tablespoon extra-virgin olive oil
Salt and freshly ground black pepper to taste

1 Give the cap a quick dunking in cold water and dry with a paper towel or cloth. Score the top of the cap with shallow incisions in a cross-hatch pattern.

2 If using a charcoal grill, prepare the fire. Shortly before grill time, brush the gills with soy sauce. Brush all surfaces of the cap with olive oil, and sprinkle with salt and pepper.

3 Place the cap on a hot grill, gill side down, and cook 2 to 3 minutes; turn and cook 2 to 3 minutes on the other side, until the mushroom surface turns a darker brown and feels pliable to the touch (similar to the feel of a medium-rare steak).

Go-Withs for Grill and Oven

These side dishes can be placed near one edge of the grill, to cook at a slower pace than the main course, or cooked in a 350- to 400-degree oven.

Cheesy Potatoes

Cut 1 large red-skinned potato into 1/8-inch-thick slices. Melt 1 1/2 tablespoons butter and grate 1 tablespoon Gruyère or Cheddar. Arrange half the slices on a piece of heavy-duty foil. Drizzle with half of the butter, add salt and freshly ground black pepper, and sprinkle on half the cheese. Top with the remaining slices, and repeat. Tightly seal the foil edges, while leaving room inside for steam to circulate. Cooking time: 20 to 30 minutes.

Veggie Skewers

Dip chunked vegetables in a vinaigrette or another marinade and thread onto skewers. Vegetables that cook in about the same length of time, such as mushrooms and bell peppers, can be alternated. If you're doing cherry tomatoes and eggplant, on the other hand, put them on separate skewers. Cooking time: 5 to 15 minutes.

Corn on the Cob

Husk the corn, and coat with butter, salt, and freshly ground black pepper. Cooking time: 10 minutes.

Pineapple Chunks

Drain canned pineapple chunks, reserving some of the juice or syrup. Combine 1 part juice with 1 part hoisin sauce and a little freshly grated gingerroot. Thread the chunks onto skewers and baste with the mixture. Cooking time (grill or broil): 10 minutes.

BEANS & GRAINS

When I asked a young, single cardiologist what he eats at home, the answer was, "Lots of beans and rice." As he has reason to know, that combination makes sense for someone who cares about nutrition but hasn't much time to cook.

A steady diet of beans and grains, whether prepared alone or together, need not be boring—because much of the world eats this way, every country and ethnic group has ideas for preparing them. Choosing just from these recipes, you can make pintos slow-cooked with a ham hock in the Southern manner, a fast Mediterrean sauté of chickpeas and spinach, or basmati rice fragrant with Indian spices.

Many single-portion cooks prefer to use canned beans, and it is easy to see why. The quantity is appropriate, the quality is decent and, best of all, they are ready to eat. But I've also included a recipe that calls for simmering a small potful of dried beans, with the prospect of delicious results.

Exotic rice varieties are nearly as easy to find and prepare as ordinary long-grained rice. Arborio and other kinds of short-grained Italian rice used to make risotto are widely available. These days basmati and jasmine rice may be imported, or grown in America and packaged in conveniently small quantities. "Super" grains such as quinoa and wheat bulgur can be cooked in much the same way as rice, and are worth a try.

Practically Speaking

About Beans

● Cook flavor into dried beans by simmering them with aromatic ingredients such as celery, carrot, garlic, and fresh herbs (especially parsley).

● To prevent skins from toughening, add salt and acidic ingredients, such as tomatoes, only to fully cooked beans.

● Drain canned beans and rinse them, to remove some salt and other additives.

● Keep in mind that a 16-ounce can typically contains 2 1/2 cups of drained beans.

● Store cooked beans, refrigerated, up to 5 days. To freeze beans, toss first with a little oil to separate the beans; pureed beans can also be frozen.

About Grains

● Buy rice and other grains in small quantities in a supermarket or health-food store, and transfer to labelled containers that seal tightly. To extend shelf life, store in your refrigerator or freezer.

● If you like sticky grains, try Japanese rice. It should be soaked, before cooking, in several changes of water.

Basmati and other Asian rice varieties sometimes need washing, as well; test a sample to see if that step is necessary.

● If you prefer rice to cook separate and fluffy, choose a long grain; Jasmine, Texmati, and Konriko Wild Pecan Rice are more interesting than regular white rice. Or, try Uncle Ben's Converted Rice.

● This simple pilaf method works for rice, barley, bulgur, kasha, and quinoa:

In a pan set over medium heat, dry toast the grain or sauté with chopped onion in butter or oil.

Add stock or water, herbs, salt, and freshly ground pepper. Bring to a boil, reduce the heat, cover, and cook until the liquid is absorbed.

Allow the cooked grain to stand, off the heat, at least 5 minutes.

● Cook only as much as you can eat at a sitting or make extra for another meal.

Leftover cooked grains can be added to a stir fry, soup, pancake batter, or croquette mixture.

Ham-Flavored Pinto Beans

Makes 2 or 3 servings   Prep: 5 minutes, plus soaking
Cook: 1 to 1 1/2 hours

1/2 pound (about 1 1/4 cups) dried pinto beans (see Notes)
1 small smoked ham hock
1 small onion, cut in half
1 bay leaf
1 teaspoon salt, or to taste
1/8 teaspoon freshly ground black pepper, or to taste

1 Rinse the beans, discarding shriveled or discolored ones and foreign matter. Put them in a medium-size saucepan, and cover with water to a level 2 inches above the beans. Soak 4 to 8 hours (see Notes).

2 Pour off the soaking water and refill the saucepan with water to a level 1 inch above the beans. Add the ham hock, onion, and bay leaf. Over high heat, bring the water to a boil. Reduce the heat to low, cover, and simmer until the beans are tender, about 1 hour; check occasionally and add water if needed.

3 Discard the ham hock, onion, and bay leaf. Using a spoon, skim off fat that has risen to the top (this is more easily done after the cooked beans are chilled several hours or overnight). Season with salt and pepper.

Cook's Notes

● Speed tip: Skip the soaking. Bring the beans to a slow boil and cook 2 minutes. Remove from the heat, cover, and let stand 1 to 2 hours before proceeding with the recipe.

● The same method can be used to cook other dried beans and legumes, including white beans, black beans, black-eyed peas, chickpeas, and lentils. Cooking times vary, depending on the variety and age of the beans. You can modify the recipe by changing the flavoring ingredients (for example, lamb neck and sage go well with white beans).

These beans look like...well, like plain old beans. We usually think of beans as an ingredient in something else, such as chili or soup. But pinto beans flavored with ham taste good enough to eat on their own, with a couple of Corn Muffins (page 167).

Spoon this colorful sauté onto rice or into a pita to make a well-balanced meal.

Chickpea and Spinach Sauté

Makes 1 generous serving   Prep: 10 minutes   Cook: 10 minutes

1 tablespoon pine nuts
2 teaspoons extra-virgin olive oil
1/4 cup finely chopped onion or shallot
1 small garlic clove, finely chopped
1/2 cup cooked chickpeas (rinsed, if from a can)
Salt and freshly ground black pepper to taste
3 cups fresh spinach, washed and roughly chopped
2 tablespoons water or broth

1 Over low heat, toast the pine nuts in a medium-size skillet (large enough to hold all the ingredients) until lightly browned, stirring often to make sure they do not burn; remove and set aside.

2 Raise the heat to medium and add the olive oil to the skillet. Cook the onion and garlic until soft and translucent, about 5 minutes. Stir in the chickpeas, and season with salt and pepper. Add the spinach and water, and cover the pan.

3 Stirring often, cook until the spinach has wilted and the chickpeas are warm, about 5 minutes. Scatter the pine nuts on top.

Notes of a Non-Cook

Charles N. Barnard's career as a travel writer has taken him all over the world. Back home in Connecticut, he likes to garden when not composing award-winning articles and books at his computer. Meal preparation is *way* down on his list of favorite pursuits.

"I'm not a cook," he protests, on being asked for a recipe. But Charles does admit to owning a crockpot, a gift from his daughter, and to using it occasionally to make chili and stews.

He starts a batch of chili by putting the contents of two cans of whole peeled tomatoes into the crockpot, and breaking them apart with a wooden spoon. In a nonstick skillet, he browns a pound and a half of ground sirloin with a finely chopped onion and, after draining any grease, stirs the meat into the tomatoes. In go chopped green pepper, some salt, cumin, and chili powder (lately, Charles has been using McCormick's Mexican-Style Chili Powder). After the chili simmers a few hours, he adds two cans of kidney beans (preferably Progresso).

Charles has also worked out a crockpot system for making lamb stew. After simmering two shoulder lamb chops in broth, he chills them overnight. The following day, he removes bones and fat, and shreds the meat with his fingers. It goes into the crockpot with carrots, onions, red-skinned potatoes, celery, and just enough water to cover it all. He might throw in a bouillon cube or a little packaged soy sauce left over from Chinese takeout; then he slow-cooks the stew until it is fork tender.

Other "non-cooking" tips from Charles:

● Steam vegetables, and season them with margarine and a spicy seasoning blend.

● Boil some angelhair pasta, and mix it with butter and Parmesan.

● Try a splash of garlic vinegar or herb vinegar on your salad.

Ann Acheson always makes a full batch of this spicy chili, but varies the way each portion is served. One day she tops a baked potato with hot chili; another day the chili is topped with grated cheese and heated in the oven; another time Ann might spread corn bread batter (made from a packaged mix) onto the single-portion casserole before baking it.

White Chili

Makes 4 servings   Prep: 10 minutes   Cook: 30 minutes

1 pound ground turkey

1 small onion, finely chopped

1 package chili mix (containing 1 spice packet, 1 thickening packet, and 1 packet red pepper flakes; see Note)

One 16-ounce can (2 1/2 cups) Great Northern, navy or other white beans, drained and rinsed

1 Over medium-high heat, cook the turkey and the onion in a medium-size skillet or saucepan. Stir often, breaking up the meat with a spatula, until the turkey turns a grayish color and the onion is translucent; drain off any fat.

2 Stir in half of the spice packet (about 1/2 cup) and 1 1/2 cups water. When the mixture comes to a simmer, reduce the heat to medium-low and cook 15 minutes. Stir in half of the thickener (about 1 1/2 tablespoons), and simmer 5 minutes longer, adding 1 cup or more water, depending on how thick you want the chili to be.

3 Add the beans and cook until they are heated through. Taste and, if you crave extra heat, add some or all of the red pepper flakes.

Cook's Note

Chili mixes are found near the canned tomatoes in most supermarkets. Because the brand recommended by Ann, Classic American Chili Mix (Texas-style), is meant to season 2 pounds of meat, I use only half of the contents to make a batch of White Chili.

variation

Vegetarian Chili: Omit the turkey. Cook the onion in 1 tablespoon vegetable oil until lightly browned, and follow the same procedure for adding the chili seasoning and thickener.

When the mixture has thickened, stir in one 19-ounce can pinto or kidney beans and one 19-ounce can black beans, drained and rinsed, and 1/2 cup corn kernels or tofu cubes.

99

Five-Minute Veggie Entrées

Tofu is not only an excellent protein source, but this soy product seems to be compatible with just about any seasoning or combination of ingredients.

Tempeh is made of cultured soybeans, sometimes in combination with grains. It has a firm, meatlike texture and tastes better than it sounds; some patties, such as those made by Lightlife, are marinated in tamari or another type of marinade. Seitan, a wheat gluten product, is another meat substitute.

Without much fanfare, any of these can be turned into a quick vegetarian entrée (see Notes for storage information).

Seasoned Tofu Cake

Cut a rectangular "cake" of tofu (about 3 ounces) and lay it on a plate. Drizzle 1/2 teaspoon of sesame oil and 1/2 teaspoon soy sauce over the cake. Sprinkle 1 teaspoon of toasted sesame seeds (page 13) and up to 1 tablespoon of chopped scallion on top. Eat the tofu cake with rice.

Tempeh or Seitan

If the patty is thick, cut it in half horizontally. Sauté in vegetable oil, turning once, until brown. Serve on a roll, with mustard, as a veggie burger. Leftover patties are good on a sandwich with mayo and spinach or tomato. Or, cube the tempeh or seitan, and use in a pasta salad or stir-fry.

Cook's Notes

● Store the tofu in water, changing it daily, and use it within a week. Tofu can also be frozen; thawed, the texture will be somewhat chewier.

● To store tempeh or seitan, follow instructions on the package. Patties in vacuum packaging have a fairly long shelf life when refrigerated or frozen.

This classic rice-cooking method works equally well with bulgur and quinoa, sometimes called "super grains" because they are so rich in protein, fiber, vitamins and minerals.

Rice Pilaf

Makes 1 serving   Prep: 5 minutes   Cook: 15 minutes

1 teaspoon butter

1 small scallion, including some of the green part, finely chopped

1/3 cup long- or medium-grain rice

1/2 cup broth or water

1/8 teaspoon salt or herb seasoning blend (omit if broth contains salt)

variations

Hoppin' John:
Gently stir 2/3 cup black-eyed peas (if canned, drain and rinse them first) into the cooked rice. Sprinkle Tabasco on top, if you like.

Bulgur Pilaf or Quinoa Pilaf: For the rice, substitute 1/3 cup wheat bulgur or quinoa. Use the same ingredients and follow the same procedure described in the main recipe.

1 Melt the butter in a small saucepan over medium heat. Cook the scallion until it is translucent. Add the rice and cook several minutes, stirring often, to lightly toast the grains and coat them with oil (do not allow them to brown).

2 Stir in the broth and the salt (if using). When the broth comes to a simmer, reduce the heat to low and cover. Simmer until the rice has absorbed nearly all the liquid, 10 to 15 minutes.

3 Allow the rice to stand, off the heat and covered, 5 to 10 minutes.

My husband, Kent, makes this aromatic fried rice as a lunch or a late-evening repast for himself and anyone else who is hungry. He uses surprisingly little oil to brown the rice and onions.

Indian-Spiced Rice

Makes 1 serving   Prep: 10 minutes   Cook: 20 minutes

2 teaspoons vegetable oil

2/3 cup chopped onion

1/4 to 1/2 teaspoon garam masala (see Notes)

1 1/2 cups cooked basmati rice (see Notes) or other long-grain rice

1 Heat the oil in a medium-size skillet over low heat. Spread the onion on the bottom of the skillet and cover. Cook the onion slowly, lifting the lid often to stir, until it is soft and translucent.

2 Stir in the garam masala. Raise the heat to medium and cook a minute or two. Stir in the rice, and spread it evenly over the bottom of the skillet.

3 Cook the rice, stirring often, until the grains are lightly browned and crisp and some of the onions brown along the edges; this step may take 10 minutes or longer.

Cook's Notes

• Garam masala is a blend of up to a dozen roasted, ground spices, including coriander, cumin, cinnamon, black pepper, and chiles. Because the strength and flavor profile can vary considerably, it is best to begin with the minimum recommended quantity and add more if needed.

• Basmati, a delicate, extremely long-grained rice, is found in Indian and Middle Eastern groceries and some supermarkets. I usually rinse imported basmati, checking for impurities, but skip this step when using American-grown basmati.

• An easy cooking method: Add 1/2 cup basmati to abundant boiling water, reduce the heat, and simmer. Start tasting after 5 minutes; as soon as the grains are tender, drain the rice.

variation

Indian-Spiced Rice with Vegetables: Top the rice with 1/3 cup diced cucumber and 1/3 cup diced tomatoes, or with 2/3 cup chopped, steamed broccoli.

102

Couscous and Red Lentils

Makes 1 generous serving   Prep: 10 minutes   Cook: 15 minutes

1/4 cup red lentils (see Notes), picked over and washed

1/2 cup vegetable, chicken, or beef broth

2 rehydrated sun-dried tomatoes, cut into small pieces (see Notes)

1/4 cup finely chopped celery

1/4 cup instant couscous (see Notes)

Salt (omit if using broth that contains salt)

Red pepper flakes (optional)

This recipe brings together two wonderful single-portion ingredients. Red lentils cook so quickly that making a small quantity is never a problem, and instant couscous, which rehydrates in minutes, is equally convenient.

Best eaten at room temperature, this grain and lentil dish can be varied in many ways. You could toss in a few toasted pine nuts and raisins, or maybe some bits of smoked turkey, or create a grain salad by adding chopped parsley and a squeeze of lemon juice. Eaten with a green vegetable, it's a meal.

1 In a small saucepan, cover the lentils with water and bring to a simmer over medium-high heat. Reduce the heat to low and partially cover the saucepan. Simmer until the lentils are tender and begin to disintegrate, about 10 minutes; drain.

2 Meanwhile, in another small saucepan, bring the broth to a simmer over medium-high heat. Add the sun-dried tomatoes and celery, reduce the heat to low and cook until the celery is barely tender.

3 Put the couscous in a soup bowl, and pour the hot broth-vegetable mixture over it; cover the bowl and let stand 5 minutes without disturbing.

4 Using a fork, fluff the couscous and gently mix in the drained lentils, sun-dried tomatoes, and celery. Taste and season with salt and red pepper flakes.

Cook's Notes

● Red (sometimes called orange) lentils and instant couscous can be found in health-food stores and, increasingly, in supermarkets. Avoid buying more expensive couscous packaged with seasonings. If you cannot find red lentils, substitute brown ones; they take only a little longer to cook.

● If the sun-dried tomatoes are purchased in dry form, rehydrate them by covering with boiling water and allowing to stand 10 minutes. Sun-dried tomatoes packed in oil need only be drained.

The risotto I make for myself seems to come out a little better than the same recipe made for several people. Indeed, it is worth noting that the best Italian restaurants cook risotto to order, one or two portions at a time.

Risotto has the reputation of being time-consuming, but it's not, particularly. You do need to stir it often, but not constantly. Take the opportunity, while keeping an eye on the risotto, to make a salad and pour yourself a glass of wine.

Risotto with Shiitakes

Makes 1 serving   Prep: 15 minutes   Cook: 20 minutes

1 1/2 cups chicken, beef or vegetable broth
1 teaspoon extra-virgin olive oil
2 teaspoons butter
1 tablespoon finely chopped shallot or onion
1 small garlic clove, finely chopped
3/4 cup cleaned, chopped shiitakes, or other mushrooms
1/8 teaspoon dried thyme, or leaves of 1 sprig
Salt (omit if the broth contains salt)
Freshly ground black pepper
1/3 cup Arborio or other short-grained Italian rice
2 tablespoons dry white vermouth
1/4 cup chopped fresh parsley
Freshly grated Parmesan

1 Bring the broth to a simmer, over low heat, in a small saucepan.

2 Heat the olive oil and half of the butter in a small skillet (about 8 inches across) over medium heat. Cook the shallot and garlic until translucent but not browned. Add the mushrooms and cook, stirring often, until they soften and reduce in size. Season with thyme, salt (if using), and black pepper. Add the remaining

teaspoon of butter, and, when it sizzles, stir in the rice. Cook a minute or two, continuing to stir, until the grains are well coated.

3 Add the vermouth, and when most of it has evaporated, ladle on enough warm broth to barely cover the rice. After that has been absorbed, stir in more broth, a little at a time. Continue stirring in broth, a little at a time, until the rice is cooked through but still slightly firm to the bite. Remove from the heat and stir in a little more broth for the risotto to "drink" while resting about 5 minutes.

4 Stir in the parsley and grate a little Parmesan over the risotto.

Cook's Note

The correct heat level is very important to success in making risotto. If the burner is too hot, the rice will cook unevenly; too slow, and it may turn gummy. I use a medium setting throughout the cooking, which is hot enough both to sauté the vegetables and to keep the risotto at a brisk (but not furious!) simmer once liquids are added.

VEGETABLES

Vegetables have everything going for them. They are quick to cook, good for you, and delicious to eat.

If possible, shop in a supermarket that sells most vegetables loose, allowing you to select the amount you need (better yet, find a good produce store or farmer's market). Nature has packaged many vegetables in sizes convenient for single-portion cooking: artichokes, carrots, green beans, and summer squash, to name a few. Baby bok choy and Japanese or Italian eggplant are downsized varieties worth seeking out.

Thinking small can help, too. Broccoli florets, sold loose, may be a more sensible buy than several stalks bound together. Buy turnips, not rutabagas, and look for the smallest cabbage.

The notion of "growing season" is fuzzier now than it used to be. At any given time, most vegetables are in season somewhere in the world—and food distributors make sure they are transported to us. Read labels and signs noting the origin of fresh vegetables, keeping in mind that the closer to your home the produce was grown, the fresher it is likely to be.

Don't rule out frozen vegetables. Peas or corn that were processed soon after harvest may have more flavor than vegetables transported from another hemisphere. A medley of frozen vegetables can add variety to your diet, as well—rather than coping with a whole head of cauliflower, you can have just a taste in a "California blend."

Cooking Vegetables

Boil

Fill a saucepan with enough water to cover the vegetable. Bring the water to a boil, add the vegetable, and cook to the desired tenderness. Drain and season.

Steam

Fill a steamer or saucepan with half an inch of water, and set it over high heat.

Place the vegetables in the steamer insert or basket, and, when the water boils, lower it into the pan. Cover and cook to the desired tenderness.

Freshly washed spinach can be steamed with no additional water; the moisture clinging to the leaves is enough.

Microwave

Pour a small amount of water or broth into a microwaveable container. Add the vegetable, season, and cover.

Microwave the vegetable at full strength, checking often, to the desired tenderness. Exceptions are corn on the cob and a whole potato, which can be wrapped in a paper towel and microwaved without additional water; husk the corn first and puncture the potato to allow steam to escape.

Roast

Slice the vegetables and toss with oil and seasonings. Roast in a single layer, uncovered, at 400 to 450 degrees. Some vegetables, such as eggplant and beets, can be punctured in several places and roasted whole.

Grill

Thread vegetable chunks onto metal skewers or pre-soaked wooden ones. Or, lay sliced vegetables flat on the grill rack or a perforated grilling pan.

For steamed vegetables with a bit of smoky flavor, wrap the slices or chunks in heavy foil; slow cookers such as potatoes should be partially precooked.

Brushing vegetables with a marinade or basting sauce adds flavor and helps them brown.

Sauté

Heat a little oil or butter in a skillet over medium-high heat. Cook the vegetables, stirring often, to the desired tenderness.

Some vegetables, such as green beans and asparagus, should be blanched (boiled briefly) before sautéing.

Roasted vegetables are so versatile that making a double portion seems sensible. You can eat the first serving as a hot side dish and, the next day, eat the rest at room temperature in one of these ways: as a salad, on a sandwich, on a pizza, chopped and mixed with any cooked pasta.

Roasted Vegetables

Makes 2 servings   Prep: 10 minutes   Cook: 30 minutes

1 red bell pepper
1 zucchini or yellow summer squash
1 unpeeled baby (Japanese or Italian) eggplant
1 medium carrot, peeled
1/4 cup extra-virgin olive oil
1 finely chopped garlic clove
1/4 teaspoon dried oregano or basil
Salt and freshly ground black pepper to taste

1 Preheat the oven to 400 degrees.

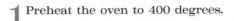

2 Cut the pepper in half and discard the seeds and stem; cut into 1-inch strips. Trim the ends of the zucchini and eggplant, and cut them vertically into 1/2-inch slices. Cut the carrot vertically into quarters.

3 Spread the vegetables in a single layer on a sheet pan. Drizzle the oil over the vegetables and sprinkle with garlic, oregano, and salt and pepper. Using your hands or tongs, turn the vegetables until they (and the pan bottom) are lightly coated with oil.

4 Roast the vegetables until fork tender, about half an hour, checking often; take out any vegetables that finish cooking before the others.

Cook's Note

Space out vegetables when preparing them for the oven—otherwise, they will steam rather than roast.

Baked Potato with the Works

Makes 1 serving   Prep: 5 to 15 minutes   Cook: 50 to 55 minutes

1 large (12-ounce) russet potato

1 to 2 cups topping (see below)

1 Preheat the oven to 425 degrees.

2 Scrub the potato. Cut a sliver off one end, to prevent pressure from building up inside the skin.

3 Bake the potato 50 to 55 minutes, until the potato feels soft when you squeeze it. Meanwhile, prepare one of the toppings.

4 Cut the potato lengthwise and lay the halves side by side. Fluff the potato pulp with a fork, and top as indicated.

toppings

Broccoli-Cheese: Blend 2 to 3 tablespoons reduced-fat sour cream or yogurt with the potato pulp; sprinkle with salt and freshly ground black pepper. Top the potato halves with 1 1/2 cups chopped, steamed broccoli (page 116) and 1/3 cup grated Cheddar. Return the potato to the oven and heat just until the cheese melts, about 5 minutes.

Chili-Cheese: Spoon 1 cup hot canned chili or White Chili (page 99) onto the potato halves. Sprinkle 1 chopped scallion and 1/3 cup Jack cheese on top, and heat in the oven until the cheese melts.

Peperonata: Sauté 1 diced Italian frying pepper or 1/2 bell pepper (any color) with 1 chopped small onion in 1 tablespoon extra-virgin olive oil until soft and lightly browned; off the heat, sprinkle on 1 teaspoon balsamic vinegar. Blend 1 tablespoon extra-virgin olive oil with the potato pulp; season with salt and freshly ground pepper; top with the sautéed peppers and onions.

Marion Cunningham, who certainly has plenty of recipes to choose from, reveals her favorite solo meal in *The Supper Book*: "I like a baked potato with olive oil and coarse salt and pepper followed by vanilla ice cream, which proves to me that money doesn't buy a good meal."

A flaky baked potato can be embellished in any number of ways. Try these toppings, or dream up your own.

Getting "Vegetized"

daniel Pinkwater, a writer and self-described fat man, has always opposed the weigh-ins, the painstaking food choices, the "fretting and failing" associated with diets. Then he noticed that eating large quantities of vegetables, mostly in the form of ratatouille, melted away some pounds while accelerating his recovery from surgery.

A regular commentator for National Public Radio, Pinkwater told listeners of "All Things Considered" that he eats ratatouille up to three times a day, with portion sizes for other foods reduced accordingly. He added, "The idea is that the highly nutritious and low-calorie ratatouille displaces more fattening foods, letting me feel full and terribly vitaminized and vigorous. Besides which, I happen to love the stuff."

In addition to "slurping it up with a spoon," Pinkwater offers these suggestions for eating the "miraculous mélange."

● Run ratatouille through the blender, with some roasted garlic, and voilá—"Such a soup!"

● Eat ratatouille cold (for breakfast, maybe?), with a squeeze of lemon juice.

● Tuck some ratatouille into an omelet or spoon it onto rice.

"You can't ruin ratatouille," insists Daniel Pinkwater. In that spirit, approach the famous Provençal stew without fear, adding something extra or leaving out an ingredient as you please.

Pinkwater's Ratatouille

Makes 4 to 6 servings Prep: 20 minutes
Cook: 1 to 1 1/2 hours

variation

Add chopped jalapeños, fresh herbs or, as Daniel Pinkwater suggests, "whatever's at hand that you think might taste good."

1/4 cup extra-virgin olive oil

1 medium or large onion, chopped

2 cloves finely chopped garlic

1 medium eggplant (about 1 pound), stemmed, peeled, and cut into chunks

2 zucchini, stemmed and cut into chunks

2 medium tomatoes or 6 plum tomatoes, stemmed and diced

1 or 2 bell peppers, stemmed, seeded, and diced

1 cup sliced shiitake or other fresh mushrooms

1 bay leaf

1/2 to 1 teaspoon seasoning blend (see Notes)

1 Heat the olive oil, over medium-high heat, in a large saucepan (preferably one with a heavy, wide bottom). Sauté the onion and garlic and, when they are transparent, stir in the eggplant, zucchini, tomatoes, bell peppers, mushrooms, bay leaf, and seasoning.

2 Cook the mixture about 10 minutes, stirring often, until the vegetables are hot. Reduce the heat to medium-low, cover the pot, and simmer for an hour or more, until the vegetables are soft. Taste and add more of the seasoning blend if needed; remove the bay leaf.

Cook's Notes

• You can use herbes de Provence, bouquet garni, Italian seasoning, or any other seasoning blend you enjoy.

• Like any good stew, ratatouille tastes even better the next day. Refrigerated, it keeps up to a week.

113

We have the Native Americans to thank for the succulent word *succotash*. Though the usual version of this dish consists of corn, squash and beans, there is some evidence that the word actually refers to only the corn kernels.

This idea pleases me, because it seems to justify throwing just about anything good together with freshly picked corn. Mild or hot peppers, tomatoes, and fresh herbs are prime candidates. If you are lucky enough to run across fresh limas or cranberry beans, put some in.

Summer Succotash

Makes 2 servings   Prep: 15 minutes   Cook: 10 minutes

2 teaspoons butter

1 large scallion with some of the green part, chopped

1 small zucchini or yellow squash, stemmed and diced

1 small Italian frying pepper, stemmed, seeded, and diced

2 ears fresh corn, husks removed

1 peeled and chopped plum tomato

Salt and freshly ground black pepper to taste

1 Melt the butter over medium heat in a saucepan large enough to hold all ingredients. Add the scallion, zucchini, and Italian pepper, cover the pan, and cook, stirring occasionally (if you think the vegetables might brown, reduce the heat).

2 Meanwhile, cut the corn kernels off the ears. When the vegetables in the saucepan are tender, stir in the corn, tomato, and salt and pepper. Cover and cook a few minutes longer, until the tomato is soft and the corn is hot.

variation

Winter Succotash: Substitute 2 cups frozen corn (or a mix of corn and limas) for the fresh corn.

These mushrooms can be eaten as a side dish, but they have lots of other uses, too: between two halves of a bun or over toast, with roast meat, mixed into pasta or rice. Ordinary white mushrooms work fine, but exotic mushrooms will have a stronger and more interesting taste.

Pan-Seared Mushrooms

Makes 1 serving   Prep: 5 minutes   Cook: 7 to 10 minutes

2 to 3 ounces portobello, crimini, or white mushrooms
1 tablespoon extra-virgin olive oil
1 tablespoon finely chopped shallot or onion
Salt and freshly ground black pepper to taste
Broth, water, or wine (optional)

1 Wipe the mushrooms with a damp paper towel, or immerse quickly in water and dry them. Trim the ends, and cut the mushrooms into thin slices.

2 Heat the oil in a medium-size skillet over medium-high heat. Cook the shallot briefly, until the pieces soften and begin to color. Add the mushrooms and cook, stirring often, until tender. Season with salt and pepper. Stir in a tablespoon or two of broth, if you like, to deglaze the pan and give the mushrooms a saucy consistency.

Glazed Baby Carrots

Makes 1 serving   Prep: 5 minutes   Cook: 10 minutes

1/4 pound peeled baby carrots
1 teaspoon butter
1 tablespoon orange juice (fresh or from a carton)
1/2 teaspoon maple syrup
Salt

1 Fill a small saucepan with enough water to cover the carrots and bring to a boil. Add the carrots, reduce the heat to medium-low, and simmer until the carrots are barely tender; about 5 minutes; drain.

2 In the same saucepan, combine the butter, orange juice, maple syrup, and a sprinkle of salt. Cook over low heat until the mixture begins to turn syrupy. Return the carrots to the pan and heat, stirring gently to coat them with the glaze.

Steamed Broccoli with Lemon

Makes 1 serving   Prep: 2 minutes   Cook: 5 minutes

6 to 8 ounces broccoli florets (see Note)
1 lemon wedge
Salt and freshly ground black pepper

1 Cut the broccoli into smaller pieces if necessary. Steam the broccoli in a steamer or saucepan (page 109) until the stems are tender, 4 or 5 minutes.

2 The broccoli is good hot or cooled to room temperature. Just before eating, squeeze the lemon juice over it and sprinkle with salt.

Cook's Note

The broccoli florets sold separately in many supermarkets are ideal for a single portion. Alternatively, use a stalk of whole broccoli, cutting the stem and florets into several pieces.

Asparagus with Sesame Seeds

Makes 1 serving   Prep: 10 minutes Cook: 5 to 10 minutes

2 teaspoons sesame seeds

4 stalks asparagus, with ends trimmed, angle-cut into 2-inch pieces

1/4 teaspoon toasted sesame oil

1 Heat the sesame seeds in a medium-size skillet over low heat until they turn light brown and give off a toasty aroma; scrape them into a small bowl. Wipe out the skillet and fill it with enough water to cover the asparagus.

2 Bring the water to a boil, and cook the asparagus pieces until crisp-tender. Drain the asparagus and toss with the sesame oil and sesame seeds.

Broccoli Rabe with Garlic

Makes 1 serving Prep: 5 minutes Cook: 10 minutes

1/4 pound broccoli rabe

1 crushed garlic clove

1 tablespoon olive oil

Salt

1 Trim the ends of the broccoli rabe. Fill a medium-size saucepan with enough water to cover the broccoli rabe, and place over high heat. When the water boils, add the broccoli rabe and cook about 3 minutes, until barely tender; drain and chop roughly.

2 In the same saucepan, cook the garlic in the olive oil over medium- high heat until lightly browned and tender. Remove the garlic and return the broccoli rabe to the pan. Sprinkle with salt, and stir frequently until it is heated through. Roughly chop the garlic and mix with the broccoli rabe.

Golden Potato Cake (Roesti)

Makes 1 serving   Prep: 5 minutes, plus time to parcook and chill the potato   Cook: 30 minutes

2 tablespoons butter

1 large potato, parboiled, peeled, and chilled several hours (see Note)

1/2 teaspoon salt

4 tablespoons milk

1 Over medium heat, melt the butter in an omelet pan or another small skillet with sloping sides, tilting it to coat the bottom and sides. Coarsely grate the peeled potato directly into the pan, spreading the shreds evenly over the bottom. Add the salt, and sprinkle the milk over the potatoes.

2 Weight the potato with a heavy pan or lid one size smaller than the skillet, compressing it into a flat cake. When the butter begins to sizzle, reduce the heat to low and cook 20 to 30 minutes, until, lifting an edge with a spatula, you see that the underside of the potato is golden brown.

3 Loosen the potato with a spatula, turn a plate upside down over the pan, and reverse to release the potato cake.

Cook's Notes

● To follow Antoinette's method, boil a large, unpeeled potato and several small ones in salted water until the small potatoes are tender. Drain and gently scrape away the skins while the potatoes are still warm. Wrap the large potato and refrigerate several hours.

● Alternatively, boil the large potato in salted water until it is easily pierced by a fork, but not completely tender, about 8 minutes.

Antoinette Cherbuliez, a Swiss-German cook, has a little trick for making roesti that allows her to indulge a passion for potatoes two nights in a row.

She boils a large potato with several smaller ones. When the small ones are tender, Antoinette eats them right away with chopped chives, salt, and Quark, a dairy product sometimes described as a cross between yogurt and cottage cheese. (For those of us who endure the misfortune of Quark-less living in America, Antoinette recommends substituting butter.)

As for the larger potato, it has cooked to just the right stage for making roesti the following day.

Easy Ways to Get Your Veggies

• Top cottage cheese with tomato pieces, carrot slices, chopped scallion or other raw vegetables; sprinkle with a seasoning blend or freshly ground pepper. Alternatively, top the cottage cheese with Marinated Cucumbers and Radishes (page 22)

• Mix a little dried onion or vegetable soup into plain yogurt or reduced-fat sour cream. Use as a dip for raw vegetables such as carrot sticks, celery, radishes, scallions, broccoli florets, Belgian endive, or the crisp inner leaves of romaine.

• Thaw frozen corn, peas, or sugar snap peas to use as salad toppers.

• Remove the tough bottom leaves of an artichoke, and trim and peel the stem. Steam the artichoke (page 109) until an outer leaf can be pulled free easily. Eat with a dipping sauce of vinaigrette or butter and lemon.

• Roughly chop kale, chard, or other greens, and boil in abundant water until wilted. Drain well and sprinkle with balsamic vinegar or lemon juice.

• Cut small, thin-skinned potatoes in half and steam until tender. Dress with butter, chopped fresh parsley, and salt and freshly ground black pepper.

• Bake a sweet potato (preferably the rounder variety with dark orange flesh) until tender. Dress with a little butter or nothing at all. For a special treat, add some pan-fried onions and crisp bacon bits.

• Lay a frozen ear of corn (or several of the shorter pieces called "coblets") on a square of aluminum foil. Add a drizzle of olive oil or a few dabs of butter, and sprinkle with an herb blend. Seal the packet and roast at 425 degrees until the cob is thawed and the corn is hot.

PIZZA

MAKING AND BAKING HINTS

Basic Pizza Dough

GREAT PIES
Potato and Pesto Pizza
White Pizza with Mushrooms and Peppers
Barbecued Chicken Pizza
Eggplant Parmesan Pizza
Smoked Salmon Pizza

FIVE-MINUTE TOPPINGS

SOLO COOK: DAVID KRAUT
Pizza Tales

Pizza is a delicious and surprisingly easy dinner to make just for yourself. Trying to turn out the same thing your local pizzeria delivers is not the point. Instead, this is a chance to try an unusual combination, such as a potato and pesto topping or eggplant Parmesan pizza, or to invent your own.

You can make your own dough following my recipe. Uncooked pizza dough is available—in a bag or rolled out, fresh or frozen—in your supermarket. Many pizzerias will sell you a pound of dough, enough for two solo pizzas, at a modest cost.

A fully cooked crust is even more convenient. Boboli, one popular brand, has onions, olive oil and Italian cheeses already cooked into the crust. And, the chewy, oniony Polish flatbread called a bialy (bee-AH-lee), best known in New York, makes a good pizza base. I also like to use "pocketless" pitas for solo pizzas.

As for toppings, it's hard to think of something that *can't* go onto a pizza crust. Search your refrigerator for chop-and-top tidbits such as the last slice of Italian salami, a marinated artichoke heart or two, a few olives, leftover spinach or broccoli.

Keep your pizza-making simple. No need for a "kitchen sink" topping; two or three ingredients that taste good together are enough.

Making and Baking Hints

About Toppings

Ideally, the topping finishes cooking at the same time as the crust. For cheeses, cured meats such as pepperoni, and tomato sauce, the timing works out fine whether you put them on an uncooked or cooked pizza crust.

Other ingredients do better when partly cooked ahead of time. Sautéing or roasting such vegetables as onions, peppers, and mushrooms reduces their bulk, eliminates excess moisture that could turn the crust soggy, and adds a protective coating of oil. Simmer sausage cubes with a little water in a covered pan to cook them and eliminate some fat; be sure to drain well.

Thawing Pizza Dough

Move the dough from the freezer to the refrigerator the day before you plan to use it. Or, thaw the dough at room temperature for two or three hours.

Shaping the Crust

Place the ball of dough on a lightly floured surface and dust the top with flour. Press the dough into a circle, and then roll it with a rolling pin until it is about 1/4 inch thick; the edges should be a little thicker than the center. Alternatively, you can press out the dough with the heels of your hands.

Baking the Pie

After breaking two pizza stones, I switched to cheap, unglazed quarry tiles that are equally helpful in producing a crisp crust. Buy enough to line your oven shelf, plus a few extras to allow for breakage.

When not in use, they stack compactly in the back of a cabinet.

The tiles are arranged in the oven when it is cold. You can place your pizza pan on top of the tiles when the oven is hot, or slide the pizza, minus the pan, directly onto the tiles.

Of course, you can forget the tiles and still make a perfectly good pizza. If you have a toaster oven, you may not even have to turn on your regular oven. It works especially well for pizzas with a precooked crust, and for reheating leftover pizza. In either case, the pizza crust should be cooked in a very hot (450 degrees) oven.

This recipe makes enough dough for three single-portion pizzas—one to eat now and two for the freezer.

Basic Pizza Dough

Makes 3 solo pizzas Prep: 15 minutes, plus rising time

1 envelope (2 1/2 teaspoons) yeast (see Note)
3 cups plus 1/2 cup unbleached all-purpose or bread flour
1 teaspoon salt
2 tablespoons plus 1 teaspoon extra-virgin olive oil

1 Fill a liquid measure with 1 cup warm (110 to 115 degrees) water. Sprinkle the yeast on top, and mix gently. A thin layer of foam should form on top within 5 minutes, indicating that the yeast is active.

2 Mix 3 cups of flour and the salt in a large mixing bowl. Add the yeast mixture and 2 tablespoons of olive oil, and mix with a wooden spoon. When most of the flour is incorporated, turn the dough out onto a lightly floured pastry or cutting board. Knead 3 to 5 minutes, adding up to 1/2 cup additional flour as necessary, until the dough is smooth and elastic (see Note).

3 Divide the dough into 3 pieces and form into balls (each will make a pizza 6 to 8 inches in diameter). Clean and dry the mixing bowl, and smear the remaining teaspoon of olive oil onto the inside. Turn one ball of dough in the bowl to coat it with oil and cover the top with plastic wrap. Wrap the other two balls in several layers of plastic wrap; label, and freeze.

4 Leave the pizza dough to rise at room temperature until doubled in bulk, 1 to 1 1/2 hours; if you make the dough more than 2 hours in advance, refrigerate it. (See page 123 for directions on shaping and baking the crust after it rises.)

Cook's Note

Use quick-rising yeast and the dough will be ready to use in 45 minutes or less.

variation

Whole Grain Pizza Dough: Use 1/2 to 1 cup whole wheat flour, rye flour, or coarse yellow cornmeal, leaving out an equivalent amount of white flour. Blend together the two grains before proceeding.

Potato and Pesto Pizza

Makes 1 solo pizza   Prep: 20 minutes   Cook: 15 minutes

Olive oil, for the pans
1 medium thin-skinned potato, sliced into 1/4-inch rounds
1/2 pound pizza dough, purchased or homemade (page 124)
2 tablespoons pesto, purchased or homemade (page 61)

1 Preheat the oven to 450 degrees.

2 Cover a small sheet pan with foil (to avoid scrubbing) and brush or spray lightly with olive oil. Lightly brush or spray oil onto the bottom of a round pizza pan (or another sheet pan).

3 Lay the potato slices in a single layer on the foil-lined pan. Cook until barely tender, about 10 minutes.

4 Meanwhile, roll or pat the dough into a round 6 to 8 inches in diameter, and transfer it to the second pan. Brush the dough with half of the pesto. Arrange the potato slices on top and brush with the remaining pesto.

5 Cook the pizza until the crust and topping are browned, about 15 minutes.

White Pizza with Mushrooms and Peppers

Makes 1 solo pizza   Prep: 10 minutes   Cook: 10 to 15 minutes

1/2 to 1 slice pancetta (Italian unsmoked bacon), or regular American bacon, cut into 1/4-inch squares

1 teaspoon extra-virgin olive oil

3 white or cremini mushrooms, thinly sliced

1/4 red pepper, cut into slivers

1/2 pound pizza dough or 1 fully cooked crust (6 to 8 inches)

1/3 cup grated Fontina cheese

1 Preheat the oven to 450 degrees.

2 Cook the pancetta in a small skillet, over medium-high heat, until lightly browned. Add the olive oil, along with the mushrooms and red pepper. Cook until the vegetables soften, about 2 minutes.

3 Roll or pat the dough into a round 6 to 8 inches in diameter, or use a fully cooked crust. Scatter the Fontina onto the crust and arrange the mushroom and pepper mixture on top.

4 Bake the pizza 10 to 15 minutes (the precooked crust will need less time) until the crust is cooked or heated through and the topping is browned.

Barbecued Chicken Pizza

Makes 1 solo pizza   Prep: 10 minutes   Cook: 10 minutes

1/2 cup diced barbecued chicken (see Note)

Up to 1/4 cup barbecue sauce

1 fully cooked pizza crust (6 to 8 inches)

2 tablespoons chopped scallions, including most of the green part

1/3 cup grated mozzarella or other mild cheese

1 Preheat the oven to 450 degrees.

2 Unless the chicken pieces are already well-coated with barbecue sauce, mix them with a little extra sauce. Spread a little more barbecue sauce onto the crust.

3 Scatter the chicken pieces and scallions on top of the crust. Sprinkle the cheese evenly over the other ingredients.

4 Bake the pizza about 10 minutes, until it is heated through and the cheese is melted.

Cook's Note

You can use leftover chicken from a barbecue restaurant or cut the meat off leftover Barbecued Chicken Thighs (page 85). Or, coat boneless, diced chicken breast with barbecue sauce and microwave, covered, until the chicken is cooked through (3 to 4 minutes).

Pizza Tales

david Kraut belongs to a generation for whom pizza holds no hint of the exotic. It is simply a given in his exuberant young life, which is filled with law school studies, song writing, performing with an a cappella group, writing op-ed pieces for newspapers, and working for inner-city economic development causes.

Growing up in L.A., David not only encountered the designer pizzas pioneered by Wolfgang Puck but met the celebrity chef, who teasingly offered him a job. At the age of eight, he was too young to seize the opportunity.

Attending Yale University, he was delighted to discover the pizzerias of New Haven, Connecticut. "They make brick-oven pizza, with a thin crust and a fantastic sauce," says David. Once, he and his date impulsively invited themselves behind the counter, and soon were saucing their own pizza. Back in his dorm, David made more prosaic pizzas. These involved smothering stale bagel halves from the cafeteria with tomato sauce, adding mozzarella and maybe some eggplant or peppers from the salad bar, and popping the student-style creation into a toaster oven.

Now, when David makes pizza in the Manhattan apartment he shares with roommates, he prefers a bialy as the crust. On top goes a 10-minute sauce he makes with fresh tomatoes, tomato paste, garlic, sugar, olive oil, and oregano. Maybe he'll add Parmesan or pineapple, or maybe not.

Occasionally David buys one of Puck's frozen pizzas, now distributed nationally, but that's pretty rare. "I shy away from premade food. If I can make it fresh, I do," he says.

Eggplant Parmesan Pizza

Makes 1 solo pizza   Prep: 15 minutes   Cook: 20 minutes

1 teaspoon plus 2 tablespoons extra-virgin olive oil

1 small Italian or Japanese eggplant

1 crushed garlic clove

Salt and freshly ground pepper to taste

1/2 pound pizza dough, purchased or homemade (page 124) or
   1 fully cooked crust (6 to 8 inches)

1/4 cup ricotta

1/2 cup loosely packed fresh parsley leaves

1/4 cup Basic Tomato Sauce (page 58) or ready-made sauce

1/2 cup grated mozzarella

2 tablespoons freshly grated Parmesan

1 Brush a sheet pan with 1 teaspoon of olive oil. Trim the ends of the eggplant and slice into 1/4-inch rounds; you should have about 1 1/2 cups, loosely packed. Rub the tops with the crushed garlic. Arrange the slices on the sheet pan, in a single layer; sprinkle with salt and pepper.

2 Brush the tops of the eggplant rounds with 1 tablespoon of olive oil. Broil until the slices are light brown. Turn them and brush on the remaining tablespoon of olive oil; brown the eggplant under the broiler.

3 Preheat the oven to 450 degrees.

4 Meanwhile, roll or pat the dough into a disk 6 to 8 inches in diameter, or use a fully cooked crust.

5 Spread ricotta on the bottom of the crust. Sprinkle with salt and pepper, and press the parsley leaves into the cheese. Drizzle the sauce onto the crust and, using a spatula, gently stroke it over the ricotta. Arrange the eggplant slices on top. Cover the top with grated mozzarella and Parmesan.

6 Cook the pizza until the crust and topping are browned, about 20 minutes.

Smoked Salmon Pizza

Makes 1 solo pizza   Prep: 10 minutes   Cook: 5 to 15 minutes

**1/2 pound pizza dough (see Notes) or 1 fully cooked pizza
crust (6 to 8 inches)**

1/3 cup soft cream cheese (see Notes)

1 teaspoon capers, rinsed

2 ounces smoked salmon, cut into ribbons

2 or 3 thin slices sweet onion

Freshly ground black pepper

1 Preheat the oven to 450 degrees.

2 Roll or pat the dough into a disk 6 to 8 inches in diameter, or use a fully cooked crust. Cook the pizza dough until browned, about 15 minutes; if using a fully cooked crust, cook only until heated through, about 5 minutes.

3 Spread the still-warm crust with the cream cheese. Press the capers randomly into the cream cheese. Arrange the smoked salmon and onion slices on top. Add black pepper to taste.

Cook's Notes

● If you make your own pizza dough, use the variation calling for rye flour (page 124).

● For easier spreading, use a soft, whipped cream cheese. If you like, use cream cheese with scallions or chives already mixed in (omit the scallions in the recipe).

Five-Minute Toppings

To make an appetizing solo pizza in almost no time, rely on condiments and leftover tidbits in your refrigerator. Until now, you may not have imagined that the moo-shu mixture sitting in a Chinese takeout carton in your refrigerator could be the key ingredient of a solo pizza. Leftover vegetables and cold cuts are equally promising.

All toppings are sized for an uncooked or fully cooked crust 6 to 8 inches in diameter.

Better Than Plain

Spread 1/4 cup tomato-based pasta sauce on the crust. Add one or more toppings: 2 sliced artichoke hearts, 3 olives cut into slivers, 5 or 6 drained and rinsed capers, 3 quartered pepperoni slices, 1/4 cup drained, canned clams or crabmeat. Sprinkle with 1 tablespoon freshly grated Parmesan.

Moo-Shu Special

Brush a few drops of sesame oil or chile oil onto the crust. Spread on 2 tablespoons hoisin sauce. Arrange up to 1 cup pork, shrimp or vegetarian moo-shu on top. Brush the top with a few drops of sesame oil or chile oil.

Broccoli Rabe

Sprinkle 1/4 cup white Cheddar cheese on the crust (omit if using a Boboli crust, which already contains cheese). Top with 1 cup of Broccoli Rabe with Garlic (page 117) left over from another meal. Sprinkle 1 tablespoon Parmesan on top.

Fresh Tomato

Brush 1/2 tablespoon olive oil onto the crust. Cut 1 small tomato or 2 plum tomatoes into 1/4-inch slices and arrange on top. Sprinkle with dried oregano, salt, and freshly ground black pepper. Scatter 1/2 cup slivers of fresh mozzarella on top.

SANDWICH & TORTILLA CREATIONS

Sandwiches can be light or filling. Cold or hot. Open-faced or not. Familiar, imaginative, or downright strange.

Preparation is usually minimal—it's the quality and mix of ingredients that make the difference between a mediocre and a great sandwich. Take that old standby, the BLT. Fry some hand-sliced, apple-smoked bacon from a good deli, add ripe tomato slices and tender Boston lettuce leaves, pile it all on challah bread with a smear of mayo, and you've got a sandwich to remember.

We normally think of sandwiches at lunchtime, but they make a good dinner, too, either alone or paired with a bowl of soup. Improvisations are a sandwich-making tradition, but the dinner sandwiches in this chapter are special enough to deserve a formal recipe.

Sandwich making can be an international adventure. Use the best breads you can find to make the Italian-style sandwiches known as panini. The newest kind of sandwich, a wrap, consists of a Middle Eastern flat bread or flour tortilla rolled around a filling. Fajitas and quesadillas make equally delicious use of tortillas.

Crusty coarse-grained bread can be as wonderful stale as fresh, when tranformed into the simple Tuscan treat called *fettunta* (elsewhere in Italy, *bruschetta* is the name for toasted bread rubbed with garlic and drizzled with olive oil). Topped with beans, it becomes a robust open-face sandwich best eaten with knife and fork.

For a single portion, a toaster or toaster oven is a more convenient heat source than the traditional wood fire, grill or oven. The choice of canned or home-cooked beans is yours, and, if you can't find great Italian bread, use an English muffin (preferred brand: Thomas'). Do use good olive oil; Coltibuono is an excellent Tuscan brand widely available in the United States.

Open-Faced Bean Sandwich

Makes 1 serving   Prep: 5 minutes Cook: 3 to 10 minutes

1 large slice (1/2-inch thick) crusty, coarse-grained Itallan bread, cut in half

1 to 1 1/2 cups cooked cannellini beans

I crushed garllc clove

2 tablespoons extra-virgin olive oil

Salt and freshly ground black pepper to taste

1 Toast the bread in a toaster until lightly browned around the edges. Meanwhile, heat the beans in a microwave or on the stove.

2 While the bread slices are still warm, rub both sides with garlic, and arrange them side by side on a plate. Spoon the beans (drained thoroughly or with a little liquid, as you like) over the bread.

3 Drizzle oil over the beans, and add the salt and pepper.

variations

Beans and Greens Sandwich: Combine 1 cup cooked, white beans (drained or with some liquid) with up to 1/2 cup cooked, seasoned spinach, kale, or other greens. Spoon over the toasted, garlic-rubbed bread and drizzle with 2 tablespoons extra-virgin olive oil.

Mushroom Sandwich: In place of beans, top the toasted, garlic-rubbed bread with Pan-Seared Mushrooms (page 115). Drizzle only 1 tablespoon of extra-virgin olive oil on top.

Paper-thin beef slices for making *bulgogi*, Korea's famous barbecued beef, can be found in some Asian markets. Otherwise, it doesn't take long to prepare the meat yourself. Grill the beef, if you like, or follow this easy stovetop method.

You can use the leftover beef on another sandwich. Or, to make another all-in-one meal, stir-fry the leftover, marinated beef with baby bok choy or snow peas, and eat with steamed rice.

Korean-Style Beef on a Bun

Makes 1 serving (with leftover beef for another meal)
Prep: 20 minutes, plus marinating time Cook: 10 minutes

1/2 pound boneless sirloin, or another tender cut

2 teaspoons toasted sesame oil

1 tablespoon reduced-sodium soy sauce

2 teaspoons rice vinegar

1 small garlic clove, minced or pressed

1 tablespoon sugar

1 Kaiser roll or soft sandwich roll (per serving)

Radicchio shreds

Sweet onion slices

1 Holding a sharp knife at a slight angle and working against the grain, cut the beef into very thin slices, no more than 1/8 inch thick (thin slices are easier to produce when the meat is partially frozen).

2 In a small, nonreactive bowl (Pyrex or stainless is good), combine the sesame oil, soy sauce, rice vinegar, garlic, and sugar. Add the beef slices, turning them to coat well with the mixture. Marinate 2 to 12 hours.

3 Heat a ridged grill pan or skillet (preferably nonstick) over high heat. When it is very hot, use tongs to lift the beef, allowing the marinade to drip back into the bowl, and lay it in the hot pan. Turn the strips as the surfaces brown. When all are cooked, remove the pan from the burner and reduce the heat to medium.

4 Split the bun halfway and, using tongs, insert half the meat. (Package the remainder in plastic wrap, label, and store in the refrigerator or freezer.)

5 Return the pan to the burner, heat briefly, and add the remaining marinade with a little water, scraping the pan with a wooden spoon to loosen any particles. Cook a minute or so, until the liquid thickens, and spoon the sauce over the meat. Top with radicchio shreds and onion slices.

A Sandwich to Remember

a s a high school student, Barbara Lydecker Crane had a passion for a unique club sandwich served at the Millburn Delicatessen, near her New Jersey home.

"It was called the 'Sloppy Joe,' but I think a better name would be the 'Millburn Sloppy Joe,' to avoid confusion with that awful, truly sloppy concoction of hamburger, tomato sauce, and squishy bun," she writes. "I have a photographic memory of how this finer version is made, gleaned from watching the lightning speed and dexterity of the deli counter guy."

Since leaving her childhood home, Barbara has become an award-winning maker of art quilts and the mother of two. Though the Millburn Sloppy Joe remains her favorite sandwich, there is nothing sloppy about the way she makes it at home. Her advice for achieving success with what she considers the world's best sandwich:

● The rye bread must be *extremely* thin.

● Precision cutting into three pieces is essential. ("It won't taste the same if you cut it differently.")

● For more verisimilitude, serve with a dill pickle. And, for total authenticity, wrap the sandwich in wax paper before you enjoy it.

Otherwise known as the "Millburn Sloppy Joe," this is a truly impressive, dinner-size sandwich.

Ham and Swiss Club

Makes 1 serving Prep: 10 minutes

1 tablespoon ketchup

1 tablespoon mayonnaise

3 slices very thin rye bread

2 ounces thinly sliced ham

2 ounces thinly sliced Swiss cheese

3 ounces (about 1/2 cup) coleslaw

1 Blend together the ketchup and mayonnaise. Spread most of the mixture on 1 side of each bread slice.

2 Layer the ham and cheese on 1 slice of rye, and place another slice (dressing side down) on top. Spread on the remaining dressing. Add the cole slaw, smoothing it to an even thickness. Top with the last piece of bread.

3 Cut the sandwich into 3 pieces, angling the knife to create a triangular middle piece.

Breads...

● Look for hard rolls and other sandwich breads sold by the piece. If you must buy a larger amount, wrap the portion not for immediate use and freeze; keep the rest, well wrapped, at room temperature.

● Rather than automatically reaching for your usual white or whole wheat, try a marbled sourdough loaf, a seven-grain bread, or one of these alternatives, ideal for sandwich making.

name	description
hard sandwich roll	taste and texture of a baguette, in a manageable size; sourdough is even better
ciabatta	crusty, sturdy bread that stands up to moist fillings
croissant	soft texture and delicate, buttery taste
ficelle	skinnier than a baguette; pumpernickel variety is worth a try
focaccia	pizzalike texture and taste; split for sandwich making; try seasoned versions such as rosemary
lavash	soft Middle Eastern flat bread; choose one with no sugar or additives for sandwich wraps
pita	comes in mini and full sizes; try variations such as onion and whole wheat

...and Spreads

Sandwich spreads and sauces keep bread from drying out and bind chopped fillings such as tuna or chicken salad. Ideally, they add another flavor dimension.

Mayo Magic

To perk up plain mayonnaise, add a sprinkle of curry powder or ground red pepper, a pinch of grated gingerroot, or a squeeze of lemon juice.

Beyond Mayo

Brush extra-virgin olive oil or Basic Vinaigrette (page 14) onto a crusty European-style bread.

Try a thin coating of storebought tapernade.

Spicy Solutions

Leave bland ballpark mustard on the supermarket shelf. Instead, choose a grainy Dijon or honey mustard.

Use dabs of salsa to enliven a sandwich.

Chutney and Such

Try a fruit sauce, such as ginger-peach chutney or whole cranberry sauce, on sandwiches filled with roast or grilled meats.

Low Fat

Spread pita, lavash, and other flat breads with hummus. Buy a good brand or mix up a batch of my favorite: Roasted Red Pepper Hummus (page 166).

Use this recipe as a model for inventing your own wraps.

Smoked Turkey Wrap

Makes 1 serving   Prep: 15 minutes

One 12-inch flour tortilla

2 tablespoons Dijon mustard, soft herb-flavored cheese (such as Boursin), or Roasted Red Pepper Hummus (page 166)

2 or 3 thin slices smoked turkey

2 or 3 thin slices provolone

1 cup torn romaine or other salad greens

1/4 cup alfalfa or radish sprouts

1/3 cup shredded carrots

1 tablespoon balsamic vinegar

1 Cover 1 side of the tortilla, out to the edges, with a thin coating of mustard. Layer the turkey and provolone slices on top, leaving a 1/2-inch border around the edges.

2 In a small bowl, toss the romaine, sprouts, and carrots with the balsamic vinegar. Scatter the vegetables over the cold cuts.

3 Fold in two parallel edges of the tortilla and, starting at the adjacent edge nearest you, roll it up.

hot tortilla tips

Microwave method: Wrap 1 or 2 tortillas in a paper towel. Microwave until hot, about 15 seconds. To warm a filled tortilla, wrap in the same way and microwave until heated through, 20 to 30 seconds.

Stovetop Method: Heat a small skillet over medium-high heat. Lay a tortilla in the pan and cook about 10 seconds, turning once or twice, until the tortilla is hot and soft. Or, in a greased skillet, lightly brown filled tortillas over medium heat, turning once. Reduce heat to low, and cover and cook the tortillas until warmed through, about 10 minutes.

Shrimp Fajita

Makes 1 serving   Prep: 10 minutes   Cook: 8 minutes

2 tablespoons vegetable oil

1 long Italian frying pepper (or 1/2 bell pepper), cut into narrow strips

1 small onion, sliced thinly

Two large (10-inch) flour tortillas

8 to 10 medium shrimp, peeled

1 lime wedge

1 cup chopped romaine and chicory, or other salad greens

2 to 4 tablespoons salsa

1 Heat 1 tablespoon vegetable oil in a medium-size skillet set over high heat. When it is very hot, sauté the pepper and onion, stirring often, until they are soft and slightly charred at the edges (take care they do not burn). Warm the tortillas (page 142); place them on a dinner plate and, using tongs, spread the pepper and onion mixture on top.

2 Heat 1 tablespoon vegetable oil in the same skillet, over high heat. When it is very hot, add the shrimp and cook a minute or two, stirring often, until they turn pink. Remove the skillet from the heat, and squeeze the lime juice over the shrimp.

3 Arrange the shrimp on the tortillas, and distribute the chopped greens and salsa over the filling. Fold in 2 parallel edges of each tortilla and, starting with the adjacent edge nearest you, roll it up.

Refried black beans are a nice change from the usual pintos. I think homemade refried beans taste better, even when you start with canned beans. If you're short on time, though, you can substitute refried beans from a can.

Black Bean Quesadilla

Makes 1 serving, with extra refried beans for another meal
Prep: 5 minutes   Cook: 25 minutes

2 tablespoons vegetable oil

1/2 cup finely chopped onion

2 cups cooked black beans

2 tablespoons salsa or picante sauce

Salt if needed

2 large (10-inch) flour tortillas (per serving)

Vegetable oil or vegetable oil spray, for the skillet

2 tablespoons Monterey Jack cheese (per serving)

1 In a medium-size skillet, heat the oil over medium-high heat, and cook the onion until lightly browned. Add the beans, spreading them evenly over the bottom of the pan. Using a potato masher or another heavy, heat-resistant object, crush the beans, stopping occasionally to stir them.

2 When most of the beans are mashed (the mixture will be somewhat chunky), add cold water little by little, stirring often, until the mixture has a thick, creamy consistency. Reduce the heat to medium-low and simmer 10 minutes; add water if the beans begin to stick to the pan.

3 Stir the salsa into the mixture. Taste and season with salt if needed. Transfer the beans to a bowl.

4 Wash and dry the skillet. Warm the tortillas, following the directions on page 142.

5 Reduce the heat to medium, and lightly coat the skillet with vegetable oil. Place 1 of the tortillas in the skillet and spread half of the bean mixture over it, leaving a 1/2-inch border around the edge (reserve the leftover beans for another meal). Sprinkle the cheese on top, and top with the other tortilla, pressing lightly to help it adhere to the filling.

6 Cook the quesadilla until lightly browned on one side. Turn and cook until the other side is browned and the cheese has melted. Let the quesadilla cool a minute or two; then cut it into 4 wedges.

Fresh Sandwich Ideas

Breads, fillings, and condiments can be fashioned into an infinite number of satisfying sandwiches. This realization was brought home to me by a hungry teenaged nephew who, after a brief but purposeful rummage through our refrigerator, improvised a burrito of cold roast pork and salsa.

Even so, it's easy to get into a rut. I often find myself mindlessly making or ordering turkey on whole wheat, with mayo and lettuce. A sensible enough choice, but how boring! If you are similarly stalled, try a few of these combinations.

Proportions are up to you, but in general, allow 4 to 5 ounces of cold cuts or other fillings per sandwich.

tuna trio

Tuna Niçoise

Toss oil-packed tuna, niçoise or other imported black olives, capers, and roasted red pepper in a garlicky vinaigrette. Transfer to a hard roll and finish with a handful of mixed greens.

Tuna-Artichoke

Dice leftover grilled tuna and mix with quartered artichoke hearts, chopped scallions, and mayonnaise. Eat on seven-grain bread.

Waldorf Tuna

Mix canned, albacore tuna with chopped apple, celery, walnuts and mayo. Pile the filling on oatmeal bread.

panini with panache

Cheese

Lay thick slices of Scamorza (smoked mozzarella) or Fontina on focaccia brushed with a vinaigrette and top with basil leaves or watercress.

Mushroom

Load both halves of a sesame bun with Pan-Seared Mushrooms (page 115) and put radicchio shreds in the middle.

Salmon and Cucumber

Spread thin slices of pumpernickel with chive-flavored cream cheese and add layers of smoked salmon and thinly sliced cucumber.

Mixed Vegetable Grill

Place grilled or roasted vegetables (page 110) on a hero roll and add a layer of overlapping provolone and mozzarella slices.

Roast Beef

Spread country-style white bread with softened goat cheese or Gorgonzola and, between the slices, put shavings of rare roast beef and watercress sprigs.

Sardine

Make an open-faced sandwich of sardines, arugula, and sweet onion slices, on pumpernickel bread spread with hot mustard or horseradish sauce.

classic variations

Meat Loaf

Arrange Mini Meat Loaf slices (page 84) on sourdough bread coated with mayo and coarse Dijon mustard, and add leaf lettuce.

Bratwurst

Split a long bun and spread with Dijon mustard, put a hot brat in the middle, and cover with thin slivers of Muenster cheese; heat in a toaster oven or under a broiler long enough to melt the cheese.

Egg

Tuck a Mexican-Style Scramble (page 151) into whole wheat pita halves, along with mixed greens.

Curried Chicken

Combine leftover, shredded or diced chicken with chopped apple and onion, and a dollop of curry-sprinkled mayonnaise, on raisin-walnut bread.

Chile-Cheese

Cover 2 pieces of whole wheat bread with slices of jalapeño Jack cheese, put a layer of sprouts in the middle, and toast in a greased skillet or toaster oven until the cheese melts.

MAINLY EGGS

EGGS, ETC.

Mexican-Style Scramble

Vegetable Frittata

Asparagus with Fried Eggs

Grits with Gruyère

French Toast

Blueberry-Croissant Concept

QUICK COMFORTS

SOLO COOK: JUDY SCHAD

Tending Goats, Making Cheese

It seems a shame to limit the perfect protein to breakfast—especially if you're the type of person who grabs a bagel or banana on the way out the door in the morning.

I feel much more enthusiastic about eating Mexican-style eggs or a vegetable frittata for dinner or a leisurely weekend brunch. The same goes for French toast with maple syrup and crisply cooked bacon.

This chapter also includes a master cheese maker's suggestions for creating a cheese plate that can easily serve as a meal. Oatmeal also makes a restorative, if unconventional, dinner for one. It can be sweetened in the usual way—unless you share my idiosyncratic taste, acquired from my mother, for hot oatmeal seasoned with butter, salt, and lots of black pepper.

Eat these eggs with warm flour tortillas, refried beans, fresh fruit, or a green salad.

Mexican-Style Scramble

Makes 1 serving Prep: 10 minutes Cook: 10 minutes

1 tablespoon butter
1/4 cup chopped onion
2 eggs
1/8 cup milk
Salt and freshly ground pepper to taste
2 tablespoons grated Cheddar or Jack cheese (optional)
1/4 cup diced tomato
1/2 to 1 fresh jalapeño, seeded, deveined, and finely chopped
2 or 3 thick corn tortilla chips, broken up

1 Melt the butter in a small or medium-size skillet over medium heat. Cook the onion about 3 minutes, until softened but still crunchy.

2 Meanwhile, break the eggs into a small bowl. Add the milk, salt, and pepper, and whisk until well blended.

3 Pour the egg mixture into the skillet. Cook, stirring often, until the eggs begin to thicken. Stir in the Cheddar, tomato, jalapeño and tortilla chips, and cook until the eggs are set but still soft.

egg tips

• If you eat eggs only occasionally, buy a small carton holding 6 or 8.

• When checking eggs before purchase, gently nudge each egg with the tip of a finger; any that stick may be cracked or broken on the bottom.

• Store eggs in the original carton, not in the plastic egg container found in some refrigerators.

This single-portion frittata looks good and tastes even better, especially when made in a small oval gratin dish. It takes very little time to assemble, especially if the vegetables are left over from another meal.

Vegetable Frittata

Makes 1 serving   Prep: 10 to 15 minutes   Cook: 25 minutes

Softened butter, for the gratin dish
1 cup sautéed or roasted vegetables (see Note)
1 egg
2 tablespoons half-and-half
Salt and freshly ground white pepper to taste
1 tablespoon freshly grated Parmesan

1 Preheat the oven to 350 degrees.

2 Butter an individual (1-cup) oval gratin dish or another small casserole dish. Spread the vegetables on the bottom of the dish.

3 In a small bowl, whisk the egg with the half-and-half. Season with salt and white pepper. Pour the egg mixture over the vegetables. Sprinkle the Parmesan on top.

4 Bake the frittata until lightly browned on top and cooked through, about 25 minutes. Allow to cool at least 10 minutes before eating.

Cook's Note

Sautéed summer squash, peppers, and onions are one pleasant combination; spinach, shallots and mushrooms are another. Or, roast some vegetables (page 110).

Asparagus Topped with Fried Eggs

Makes 1 serving   Prep: 10 minutes   Cook: 5 to 10 minutes

6 to 8 asparagus stalks, ends trimmed
2 teaspoons butter
1 or 2 eggs
Salt and freshly ground pepper to taste
1 tablespoon freshly grated Parmesan

This classic Italian all-in-one should be eaten with crusty bread, to catch the delicious sauce created when the egg yolk mingles with the butter and cheese.

1 Bring 1/2 inch water to a boil in a pan large enough to hold the asparagus (either horizontally or vertically). Place the asparagus in a steamer insert, lower into the pan, and cover. Steam until barely tender, about 5 minutes (test by cutting off and tasting a piece of the stalk).

2 Drain the asparagus and place on an ovenproof plate. Coat the asparagus with 1 teaspoon of the butter, and place it in an oven set on warm.

3 Melt the remaining butter in a small skillet over medium heat. Crack the egg over the skillet, letting the contents slide into the hot butter. Cook until the white turns opaque and begins to firm up, about 1 minute; using a spatula, turn the egg. Season with salt and pepper, and cook a few seconds longer, until the white is cooked through but the yolk is still slightly runny.

4 Lay the egg on top of the asparagus, and sprinkle the Parmesan on top.

Cook's Notes

● After you have made this dish a time or two, speed up the preparation by frying the egg while you steam the asparagus.

● Microwave method: Combine the asparagus with a little water in a microwaveable dish, cover, and microwave until the spears are tender (3 to 4 minutes).

153

Tending Goats, Making Cheese

Judy Schad's day begins at 5:30 A.M. with a trip to the barn to check on her herd of 200 goats. "During the kidding season, especially, I want to see if anyone has a problem," she says. She watches as the milking gets under way, turns on the boiler in the cheese plant, returns to the house to do paperwork. By early afternoon the fresh chèvre is ready for packaging under her Capriole, Inc., label, while other cheeses have gone to the dry room for aging.

This arduous routine has brought well-deserved recognition to Judy, including a "Best of Show" award from the American Cheese Society and induction into the French guild of cheese makers. Mastering the art of cheese making is not unlike cooking, she says. "There comes a day when you throw the measuring spoons out the window and just do it. At some point, I knew I could make goat cheeses as good as the ones I had tasted in France."

A perfect cheese with a perfect wine beats chocolate truffles any time, in Judy's view. On a summer day, she recommends fresh goat cheese at room temperature, with a chilled sauternes. When there's a chill in the air, consider nibbling a slice of Stilton with a glass of port.

More of Judy's thinking on cheese plates:

● Pair cheese with seasonal fruit—fresh figs, a ripe pear or apple, berries, or sweet grapes.

● Eat fresh goat cheese drizzled with extra-virgin olive oil and herbs, crusty bread, wonderful olives, and maybe a tomato on the side.

● Try chutney with "big cheeses" such as blues. Spiced, toasted pecans or walnuts are a good match, as well.

Grits with Gruyère

Makes 2 servings   Prep: 15 minutes   Cook: 40 minutes

Butter, for the gratin dish

1/3 cup regular grits (not instant)

1/2 teaspoon salt

1/3 cup Gruyère

1/8 teaspoon freshly ground white pepper

1 egg

1 tablespoon butter, melted

1/3 cup milk

1 Preheat the oven to 400 degrees.

2 Coat a small casserole or two 1-cup oval gratin dishes with butter. In a medium-size saucepan, bring 1 2/3 cups water to a boil. Stir in the grits and the salt. When the water returns to a boil, reduce the heat to low and cover. Simmer 10 minutes, stirring occasionally. (Alternatively, the grits can be microwaved, following package instructions.) Let the cooked grits stand until barely warm. Stir in the Gruyère and white pepper.

3 In a small bowl, combine and whisk the egg, melted butter, and milk. Stir the liquid mixture into the cooled grits, and transfer to the gratin dish.

4 Bake 30 minutes, until the liquid has been absorbed and the top is firm. Broil just long enough to brown the top.

Cook's Note

To reheat leftover grits casserole, microwave at full power until hot, about 1 minute.

In the rolling hills of southern Indiana, only a stone's throw from Kentucky, springtime brings the annual ritual of the Derby breakfast. "You eat country ham, sweetbreads, cheese grits, and pickled Jerusalem artichokes along with things of the season, such as fresh morels and new potatoes," says cheese maker Judy Schad.

Even when you are making a solo meal, not a buffet, you can do a modified version of the Derby breakfast—any time of day. Scramble a couple of eggs and put them on a plate with a slice of country ham or prosciutto and these delicious grits, which Judy describes as "fondue with grain."

French toast is easy to make on the spot. But, if you like the idea of ready-to-heat slices or have a loaf of bread beginning to go stale, make a batch for the freezer. Top your French toast with maple syrup, fresh fruit, or preserves.

French Toast

Makes 1 large serving   Prep: 5 minutes   Cook: 5 minutes

1 egg
1/2 cup milk
1 dash cinnamon or nutmeg
1/4 teaspoon vanilla
2 large, thick (1-inch) slices bread
1 tablespoon butter

1 Combine the egg, milk, cinnamon, and vanilla in a Pyrex pie plate or other wide, shallow container, and whisk until well blended. Soak the bread slices on both sides, and let stand until the liquid is absorbed, about 5 minutes.

2 Over medium-high heat, melt the butter. When it sizzles, cook the bread slices, turning once, until brown on both sides.

variations

Freezer French Toast: Double or triple the ingredient quantities. After dipping, place the bread slices on a rimmed baking sheet; spoon any leftover egg mixture over them. When the bread has absorbed the egg mixture, place the uncovered baking sheet in the freezer. Wrap the frozen slices individually in plastic wrap, transfer to recloseable plastic bags, and return to the freezer.

To heat: Remove the desired number of slices from the bag. Spread softened butter on both sides and on the bottom of an ovenproof pan (or coat the latter with an oil spray). Bake in a 450-degree oven or toaster oven about 15 minutes, turning once, until the slices are brown.

Stuffed French Toast: Using a small, serrated knife, make a pocket in 2 thick slices of whole wheat or pumpernickel bread by cutting through the top crust almost to the bottom crust, leaving a 1/2-inch border on three sides. Insert thin slices of Swiss cheese and ham. Omitting the vanilla and cinnamon from the egg mixture, follow directions in the main recipe for dipping and cooking the slices.

This kind of grilled sandwich, known in France as a *croque monsieur*, can be picked up with the fingers. It is equally delicious when drizzled with maple syrup, and eaten with knife and fork.

Blueberry-Croissant Concept

**Makes 2 servings   Prep: 15 minutes, plus standing time
Cook: 20 to 25 minutes**

Butter, for the gratin dishes

1 croissant (can be stale)

1 egg

1/2 cup half-and-half

2 tablespoons sugar

1 or 2 drops almond extract (optional)

1 cup blueberries, picked over and washed

2 tablespoons sliced almonds

1 Preheat the oven to 350 degrees.

2 Butter 2 individual 1-cup gratin dishes or a small casserole dish. Using your fingers, shred the croissant. In a small bowl, whisk the egg, half-and-half, sugar, and almond extract until well blended.

3 Line the gratin dishes with half of the shreds (from the interior of the croissant). Arrange the blueberries in a single layer. Divide the egg mixture between the dishes. Arrange the croissant crusts on top, and sprinkle on the almonds. Gently press down with the flat of the hand to submerge the lower layers in the egg mixture. Let the mixture stand at least 15 minutes (or, refrigerated, up to 12 hours).

4 Bake the blueberry-croissant mixture 20 to 25 minutes. Test by pressing the mixture away from the side of the dish with a spoon; if no liquid is visible, it is ready.

This little blueberry number is based loosely on one of the egg dishes served by innkeeper Marge Rumsey to grateful guests of her Buttermilk Falls Bed and Breakfast in Ithaca, New York. Asked for details of its preparation, she said, "Oh, I don't do recipes. I do concepts!"

Though Marge normally cooks for a crowd, her blueberry concept adapts easily to serve one, with some left to eat later. It tastes good alone, and even better with ice cream.

Quick Comforts

Oatmeal with Extras

Using old-fashioned oats (not instant) or Irish oatmeal, follow the directions on the package for making one serving. After removing from the heat, add one or more mix-ins: dried Mission figs, dates, or apricots cut into small pieces; raisins or dried cranberries; honey, brown sugar or maple syrup to taste; pecans, walnuts, or pine nuts; a touch of cinnamon or nutmeg.

No Better Bagel

Lightly toast a plain or onion bagel. Spread the halves with cream cheese, and drape thin slices of smoked salmon (preferably lox or Nova) on top.

Pancakes Plus

Mix a little wheat germ or whole wheat flour into 1 portion of pancake mix, or buy a good whole grain pancake mix. To make a more interesting batter, add applesauce and cinnamon, or mashed banana and chopped pecans.

Beef Hash and Eggs

Heat a can of good-quality corned beef hash. Meanwhile, cook 1 or 2 eggs "over easy" in a little butter. Top the hash with the eggs.

Grapefruit and Rye Toast

Halve a grapefruit and run a paring knife around the fruit segments to free them. Smear a little honey on top of the halves and heat under a broiler 5 minutes. Follow the warm grapefruit with a second course of hot, well-buttered rye toast.

SNACKS & SWEETS

SAVORY SNACKS

Microwave Nachos

Seasoned Pecans

Cheese Popcorn

Roasted Red Pepper Hummus

Corn Muffins

SWEET TREATS

Mixed Fruit Smoothie

Chutney Apple Crisp

Granola Deluxe

Currant Cookies

Spiced Pickled Grapes

SPEEDY SNACKS

SOLO COOK: ANTONIA ALLEGRA

Singular Delights

When it comes to treats, sweet or savory, we all have our quirks. One day, I crave the pungent snap of pickled peperoncini or okra. Another, I long for a luscious smear of Gorgonzola or herbed goat cheese on a cracker. For me, "crunchy" is an entire category filled with desirable alternatives: rice cracker tidbits, chilled celery sticks, dry-roasted nuts, and cheese popcorn, to name a few.

If I have a perfectly ripe pear, nectarine, or plum in my kitchen, it won't last. A pleasant chocolate interlude might center on a hazelnut chocolate bar or Mallomars, my favorite cookie brand. And, I admit to a fondness for the fascinating "fish eyes and glue" texture of tapioca pudding.

Some snacks and sweets in this chapter are assembled in a few minutes, but others take longer. Eat a carrot while you wait, and look forward to having some corn muffins or currant cookies on hand.

Microwave Nachos

Makes 1 serving   Prep: 5 minutes   Cook: 20 seconds

1/4 cup refried beans
10 corn tortilla chips, baked or regular
10 thin slivers Jack cheese
5 jalapeño slices, cut in half (see Note)

1 Spread refried beans on the tortilla chips. Lay a sliver of Jack cheese on top of each.

2 Arrange the nachos in a single layer on a microwaveable plate. Microwave 15 to 20 seconds, until the cheese melts and the nachos are hot.

Cook's Note

Fresh jalapeños are often sold loose in the produce department, allowing you to buy just one or two. Otherwise, buy a small jar of vinegared jalapeños, which will keep indefinitely in the refrigerator.

Olive oil brings out the rich flavor of the pecans, while maple syrup adds a hint of sweetness. Though I usually make these seasoned pecans in large batches for holiday gifts, this recipe is sized for one lucky person.

Seasoned Pecans

Makes 1 cup   Prep: 5 minutes   Cook: 15 to 20 minutes

1 teaspoon maple syrup
2 teaspoons extra-virgin olive oil
1 cup pecans
Kosher salt

1 Preheat the oven to 300 degrees.

2 Combine the maple syrup and olive oil in a small microwaveable bowl. Microwave until the liquids blend easily, about 20 seconds, or warm over low heat on top of the stove.

3 Line a small baking sheet with foil and spread the pecans in a single layer. Drizzle the liquid mixture over the nuts, and push the pecans around with a spatula until all are coated. Sprinkle with kosher salt.

4 Toast the pecans 15 to 20 minutes, until lightly browned and crisp, checking often to make sure they do not burn. Store any you do not eat immediately in a tightly sealed container.

in praise of air popping

Air popping allows you to control the nature and amount of oil and seasonings added to popcorn, and to make the exact amount you want (1/3 cup uncooked corn is a typical single serving). If you eat popcorn often, consider buying an air popper.

Features to look for: a vent permitting steam to escape; a thermostat that automatically shuts off the heating element at the end of the popping cycle; and a Popcorn Institute Seal of Quality Performance.

You can eat air-popped corn completely unseasoned, but that's not much fun. Instead, toss it with a little melted butter or warm vegetable oil, seasoned with salt and ground red pepper or with an herb seasoning blend.

I love the taste of cheese popcorn, but hate finding most of the cheese at the bottom of the bag or bowl. After a few tests, Nancy Radke, a recipe developer who is also marketing and communications director for the Parmigiano-Reggiano Consortium, solved the problem. The steam inside the bag, together with the shaking action, create a delicious bond between popcorn and cheese.

Cheese Popcorn

Makes 1 or 2 servings   Prep: 3 minutes   Cook: 5 minutes

1/4 to 1/3 cup finely grated Parmigiano-Reggiano cheese
Dash of ground red pepper
1 bag microwave popcorn (see Note)

1 Combine the cheese and red pepper. Pop the corn according to directions.

2 Open the bag, taking care not to burn your fingers, and add the cheese mixture. Roll the top of the bag shut and shake the bag for 1 minute.

Cook's Notes

● This recipe was tested with Orville Redenbacher's butter- and natural-flavored popcorn. Because the cheese naturally contains sodium, you may want to consider choosing a low-salt or no-salt popcorn.

● Store leftover popcorn in a recloseable plastic bag to enjoy later.

Warm pita triangles spread with hummus make a good snack or, with soup or salad, a light meal. You can also use this salmon-colored hummus as a low-fat, big-flavor spread for a roast beef or turkey sandwich.

Roasted Red Pepper Hummus

Makes 1 1/3 cups   Prep: 15 minutes

1 1/2 cups cooked chickpeas

2 teaspoons tahini (sesame seed paste)

3 tablespoons lemon juice

1/2 cup (about 3 ounces) ready-made roasted red pepper, or 1 freshly roasted red pepper (see Note)

1 small garlic clove

1/3 teaspoon salt

1 Combine the chickpeas, tahini, lemon juice, roasted red pepper, garlic, and salt in a food processor. Puree until the mixture is fairly smooth, with specks of red pepper, scraping down the sides of the bowl once or twice.

2 If the hummus seems too thick, add a tablespoon or two of water and pulse until it is incorporated.

Cook's Notes

● Split the pepper in half and place on a foil-lined pan. Broil 6 inches from the heat source until the skin is blackened. Transfer the pieces to a paper bag, fold the top shut, and cool the pieces (the steam helps separate the skin from the flesh). Pull away the blackened skin.

● Refrigerated, the hummus will keep at least a week, although it may lose some flavor toward the end. You can also freeze some.

On their own, corn muffins make a great "any time" snack. They are also nice to eat with beans or a stew.

Corn Muffins

Makes 12 muffins   Prep: 15 minutes   Cook: 20 to 25 minutes

variation

Add 1/4 cup corn kernels, fresh or frozen and thawed, to the batter.

Softened butter, for the muffin tin

3/4 cup cornmeal

3/4 cup unbleached all-purpose flour (see Note)

2 tablespoons sugar

1 tablespoon baking powder

1/2 teaspoon salt

1 egg

1 cup milk

2 tablespoons butter, melted

1 Preheat the oven to 425 degrees. Generously butter the muffin tin.

2 Combine the cornmeal, flour, sugar, baking powder, and salt in a medium-size bowl large enough to hold all the ingredients; mix gently with a whisk. In a small bowl, whisk the egg together with the milk and butter.

3 Pour the liquid ingredients into the larger bowl, and with a few strokes of a spatula, mix them with the dry ingredients (do not overmix).

4 Spoon the batter into the muffin tin, filling each compartment about 3/4 full. Bake until the muffins are lightly browned, about 20 minutes. Allow the muffins to cool 5 minutes in the tin before transferring them to a rack.

Cook's Notes

● To measure: Spoon the flour and cornmeal into a measuring cup; do not pack.

● To freeze: Wrap the muffins individually in plastic wrap and place them in one or more recloseable plastic bags. Thaw the desired number of muffins at room temperature or in the microwave.

This smoothie is a juicy slush, thickened a little by the banana. But a smoothie can also be a rich shake, depending on the ingredients you choose.

Soft, fully ripe fruit is a good starting point: Berries, melon, pineapple, papaya, mango, and peaches are all wonderful. If the fruit is fresh, so much the better. But, because the mixture will be pureed, flavor is more important than texture—so you can use frozen berries or papaya pieces from a jar if you like.

Mixed Fruit Smoothie

Makes 1 large (16-ounce) serving   Prep: 10 minutes

1/2 cup apple juice or cider
1 small banana, peeled and cut into chunks
1 ripe peach, peeled and sliced
3 strawberries, cut in half
1/2 cup ice cubes
Sprinkle of cinnamon

Combine the apple juice, banana, peach, strawberries, ice cubes, and cinnamon in a blender container. Blend on high speed until the mixture is smooth and a bit frothy on top.

more smooth ideas

Fruit-Yogurt Shake: Omit the banana and ice cubes, and combine the other ingredients with 1/2 cup frozen vanilla yogurt.

Coffee-Banana Shake: Blend 1 peeled banana, cut into pieces, with 1 large scoop of coffee ice cream and 1/2 cup milk.

Citrus Cooler: Blend 1 cup orange juice with 1 large scoop lemon sorbet (Häagen-Dazs makes a good one), 1 tablespoon lime juice, and 1/2 cup ice cubes.

I love apples and chutney, but never thought of putting the two together until I read Rozanne Gold's inventive cookbook *Recipes 1-2-3*. This baked apple with a crisp topping, an adaptation of her recipe, can be dessert—or, without the ice cream and granola, a pleasing companion to a pork chop or slice of ham.

Chutney Apple Crisp

Makes 1 serving   Prep: 8 minutes   Cook: 50 minutes

1 large cooking apple (see Notes)
1 tablespoon mango chutney (see Notes)
1 large scoop vanilla ice cream or yogurt (optional)
2 tablespoons granola, purchased or your own (page 170)

1 Preheat the oven to 400 degrees.

2 Cut 1/4 inch off the top of the apple. Using a corer or small, sharp knife, cut out the core, taking care not to cut through the bottom (if you do, plug the hole with a bit of apple).

3 Fill the cavity with chutney and smear the top with a thin coating of the chutney syrup. Set the apple upright in a small baking pan, surrounded by 1/2 inch of water.

4 Bake 45 to 50 minutes, until the apple is soft but not falling apart; as it cooks, spoon the juices over the apple once or twice. Transfer the apple to a shallow soup bowl, and allow it to cool 15 minutes. Top with a large scoop of vanilla ice cream, if using, and sprinkle the granola over both.

Cook's Notes

• Red Delicious, Golden Delicious, Rome, and Granny Smith are some apple varieties recommended for baking. You can also use an Asian pear.

• Major Grey's is a good and widely available brand.

Granola Deluxe

Makes 11 to 12 cups (1 1/2 pounds)   Prep: 15 minutes
Cook: 1 hour

Vegetable oil or oil spray, for the sheet pan

1/3 cup vegetable oil

1/2 cup honey

1 teaspoon vanilla

5 cups regular oatmeal (not instant)

1 cup wheat germ

1 cup grated coconut

1/2 cup powdered milk

1 tablespoon cinnamon

1/2 cup chopped pecans or walnuts

1 cup dried cranberries or raisins, or a mixture

1 Grease a sheet pan lightly with vegetable oil. Over low heat, in a small saucepan, warm the vegetable oil with the honey and vanilla until they can be blended easily (or heat them in a microwave).

2 Combine the oatmeal, wheat germ, coconut, powdered milk, cinnamon, and nuts on the sheet pan. Add the liquid mixture, and, using a wooden spoon, stir gently until the dry ingredients are coated.

3 Set the oven at 250 degrees and bake the mixture about 1 hour, stirring occasionally, until the granola is light brown. Stir in the dried fruit, then cool.

Cook's Note

Stored in an airtight container, the granola will stay fresh several weeks. Alternatively, you can freeze some in recloseable plastic bags.

My dad enjoys eating breakfast on his deck, a habit encouraged by the mild climate of East Texas. Sometimes he is joined by my mom or a guest, but more often than not, it's just him among the pines with a crisp morning newspaper, a mug of coffee, and, to make life perfect, an artfully composed bowl of cereal.

First there's a sturdy base of bran cereal or shredded wheat, then a layer of banana slices and, as the pièce de résistance, a sprinkling of granola. You can buy granola, of course, but sometimes it's nice to make your own to eat for breakfast or as a topping for ice cream and other desserts.

Speedy Snacks

- Rice cakes or graham crackers spread with peanut butter

- Good white bread spread with softened chocolate (a French treat)

- Frozen grapes or a peeled, frozen banana

- Trader Joe's Dark Chocolate-Covered Espresso Beans

- Cottage cheese with scallions or a Boursin-style cheese, scooped up with endive leaves or whole grain crackers

- Fritos dipped in soft cream cheese mixed with a little jalapeño jelly or Pickapeppa Sauce

- Mediterranean black olives marinated in a mixture of olive oil, lemon juice, garlic, and red pepper flakes

- Pickled herring on pumpernickel bread

- Thick (but fat free) sourdough pretzels

- A mug of hot beef or chicken bouillon with saltines

- A persimmon (scooped with a spoon), slices of starfruit, or some other interesting fruit

- Chocolate ice cream sprinkled with wheat germ

- Triscuits with thin Gouda slices, broiled until the cheese melts

- A cantaloupe wedge filled with vanilla ice cream

- Chilled dill pickles, pickled okra, or pickled Italian peppers

- Pistachios or peanuts fresh out of the shell

- Hard-cooked eggs with salt and pepper, and bread and butter

- Frozen chocolate confections, with Dove Bars topping the list

Why should a solo cook miss out on the pleasure of good homemade cookies? You can share some with friends, or freeze some to replenish your cookie jar.

Whenever I make these small, buttery cookies, I think of Richard Glavin, who teaches culinary classes at The New School for Social Research, in New York. Demonstrating how to make these, he confided that they are his favorite cookie—and no wonder.

Currant Cookies

Makes about 6 dozen cookies   Prep: 30 minutes
Cook: 10 minutes (per pan)

Butter, for the sheet pan
2 sticks (1/2 pound) butter, softened
1 1/4 cups sugar
1 egg
1 teaspoon vanilla extract
2 cups all-purpose, unbleached flour (see Notes)
1/4 teaspoon salt
1 cup currants

1 Preheat the oven to 350 degrees.

2 Butter a large sheet pan, coat it with an oil spray, or line it with parchment paper.

3 In the large bowl of an electric mixer (see Notes), cream the butter and sugar on low to medium speed until the mixture is pale yellow and fluffy. Turn off the machine and scrape down the sides of the bowl. Add the egg and the vanilla, and blend well.

4 Combine the flour, salt, and currants in a medium-sized bowl. Add to the other ingredients and mix on low to medium speed only until incorporated. Transfer the mixture to a 1-gallon recloseable plastic bag or to a smaller bowl (cover with plastic wrap). Chill thoroughly (see Notes).

5 Pull off small bits of the chilled batter and, between your hands, roll into balls the size of hazelnuts. Place the balls 1 1/2 inches apart on a baking sheet. Flatten each one with your thumb (the dough edges will be slightly higher than the depressed middle). Bake until the cookies turn brown around the edges, about 10 minutes. Transfer the cookies to a rack to cool.

Cook's Notes

● Measure the flour by spooning into a measuring cup; do not pack down.

● In a stand-alone mixer, use the paddle attachment.

● Chill the dough at least 2 hours in the refrigerator. Or, if you are in a hurry (and I always am), chill it in the freezer.

● In a well-sealed container, these cookies will keep at least 10 days. You might store some in the freezer and transfer to your cookie jar as needed. Or, you can divide the dough into smaller batches to freeze and bake whenever you like.

Singular Delights

for more than a decade, Antonia Allegra has lived in a "tree house" in the Napa Valley. She describes her home this way not because it actually is perched high in the branches, but because the tree-filled views seen through every window create that illusion.

Though Toni married recently, her husband lives in another city, so she continues to eat alone most weekdays. "I love cooking for myself almost as much as cooking for others," she says.

During her working hours as a culinary professional, Toni limits snacks to carrot sticks or jicama slices with a squeeze of lime. But, when the sun goes down, she treats herself (and any guests she might have) to delectable pre-dinner tidbits made with fruit, cheese, and nuts.

Homemade pickled grapes go well with a glass of Napa Valley wine. Walnuts tossed and toasted with olive oil, salt, ground red pepper, and dried rosemary are another favorite. Toni also loves a slice of walnut bread spread with Cambozola cheese and a drizzle of honey. She buys her Cambozola by the wedge, but it's easy to make a version of this cheese blend, following her directions: Blend together 1 part Gorgonzola with 2 parts Camembert (with the rind removed), and keep it in a crock to use as a spread.

When local fresh figs are available, Toni spreads Cambozola onto a split pita and adds a layer of unpeeled figs, cut in quarter-inch rounds. She finishes the baked personal-size pizza with a touch of honey. Dried figs stuffed with walnuts are another sweet-and-savory treat that evokes the Christmas tables of her childhood. "Dip the fig 'sandwich' into port or melted chocolate if you like," she says.

Antonia Allegra keeps these cinnamon-spiced grapes on hand to eat with seasoned nuts, with a sandwich, or all alone. "If you're going to someone's house for dinner, tie a ribbon around one of the jars. It makes a great little gift," she adds.

Spiced Pickled Grapes

Makes 4 cups   Prep: 15 minutes   Cook: 10 minutes

4 cups red or green seedless grapes, stemmed and washed
1 1/2 cups sugar
1 cup white vinegar (distilled, white-wine or rice)
Four 3-inch cinnamon sticks
2 tablespoons minced onion

1 Place the grapes in 4 half-pint canning jars or in a quart jar. In a small saucepan, combine the sugar, vinegar, cinnamon sticks, and onion. Over high heat, bring the mixture to a boil. Reduce the heat to low, and simmer 5 minutes.

2 Let the mixture cool, off the heat, for 5 minutes. Divide the cinnamon sticks among half-pint jars (or put all of them in a 1-quart jar), and pour the liquid over the grapes. Seal the jars and refrigerate at least 8 hours before eating.

Cook's Note

The pickled grapes will keep, refrigerated, up to 1 month. To prevent green grapes from darkening, place the jars in individual brown bags, fastened at the top with rubber bands.

index

183